FOREVER WARS

BOSTON REVIEW

Publisher & Coeditor-in-Chief Deborah Chasman

Coeditor-in-Chief Joshua Cohen

Executive Editor Matt Lord

Associate Editor Cameron Avery

Contributing Editors Thomas Ferguson, Adom Getachew, Jake Grumbach, Lily Hu, Robin D. G. Kelley, Becca Rothfeld, & Simon Torracinta

Editorial Assistant Juliana George

Columnists Olúfẹ́mi O. Táíwò, David Austin Walsh

Associate Publisher Jasmine Parmley

Finance Manager Anthony DeMusis III

Board of Advisors Derek Schrier (Chair), Margo Beth Fleming, Archon Fung, Deborah Fung, Larry Kramer, Richard M. Locke, Jeff Mayersohn, Scott Nielsen, Robert Pollin, Rob Reich, Hiram Samel, Kim Malone Scott, Brandon M. Terry, & Michael Voss

Print and Cover Design Rest Design

Cover Art Edel Rodriguez

Forever Wars is *Boston Review* issue 2026.2.

"War's Queer Face" is adapted from *The Queer Face of War* by J. Lester Feder, published by Verlag Kettler in February 2026. Photographs copyright J. Lester Feder, courtesy of Outright International.

Supported in part by generous grants from the Open Society Foundations and the William and Flora Hewlett Foundation.

Printed and bound in the United States by Sheridan.

Distributed by Haymarket Books (www.haymarketbooks.org) to the trade in the U.S. through Consortium Book Sales and Distribution (www.cbsd.com) and internationally through Ingram Publisher Services International (www.ingramcontent.com).

Image on pages 34 and 35: AP Images

To become a member, visit bostonreview.net/memberships.

For questions about donations and major gifts, contact Jasmine Parmley at jasmine@bostonreview.net.

For questions about memberships, email members@bostonreview.net.

Boston Review
PO Box 390568
Cambridge, MA 02139

ISSN: 0734-2306 / ISBN: 979-8-99374943-3

CONTENTS | SPRING 2026

REVIEWS

EDITORS' NOTE

A DECADE AGO, Donald Trump was clear. "Obviously, the war in Iraq was a big, fat mistake," he declared at a Republican presidential debate. "George Bush made a mistake. . . . We should have never been in Iraq. We have destabilized the Middle East." It was not a passing sentiment. "I'm not going to start wars," he reiterated on election night in 2024.

This February, the United States and Israel started a war with Iran, massively destabilizing the Middle East. In a roundtable discussion in this issue, four scholars of Iranian history and politics assess the shifting justifications, obvious miscalculations, and growing geopolitical, economic, and human toll. "We have seen different rationales," Peyman Jafari argues, "because making the real reason explicit would have been unhinged, even for Netanyahu and Trump." At bottom are "imperial anxieties" in the face of a changing global order. According to Manijeh Moradian, the United States and Israel "want the world to accept that this is the way it is, that they can do whatever they want." The Iranian people, already the targets of brutal repression by their own government, are caught in between.

The human face of war runs throughout the issue. In a diary from March, an art director in Tehran bristles with hatred as a Basiji guard approaches her car. She had always viewed the Basij as the oppressive face of the Islamic Republic, yet the young man warns her that parking too close to their checkpoint is risky: it's a likely target for drone strikes. The gesture startles her. "It was as if in a brief moment our relationship changed," she writes. Other essays in the issue—dispatches from Lebanon, Iraq, and the West Bank, as well as a photo essay from Ukraine—further illuminate how a sense of common humanity can emerge in unlikely circumstances, and the powerful forces that can shatter it.

What can be done? As columnist Olúfẹ́mi O. Táíwò argues, the U.S. ruling class seems captivated by the fantasy that it can hide from the destruction it unleashes, whether in apocalypse bunkers or White House ballrooms. When consequences do catch up with elites, their shock reveals they are "appalled . . . to live in the same world as the rest of us." We need to end their reign of impunity by using the power of the law to hold them to account.

Elsewhere, Harsha Walia urges that calls for "abolishing ICE" get something fundamentally wrong: to end the violence at the heart of today's fascist politics, we need to reject borders themselves. Farah Bakaari draws lessons from Somaliland's anticolonial struggles, which she argues have been betrayed by conflating self-determination with statehood. Two essays about novelists explore the role of imagination in a world increasingly hostile to it (Holter and Dunne), and two others challenge tech's grip on our ideas about human creativity and the good life (Rubin and Grue).

Finally, on the 250th anniversary of the Declaration of Independence, David Waldstreicher revisits the long debate over the meaning of the American Revolution. Is it defined by its most undemocratic features, closing the nation off to change? Waldstreicher thinks not: the nationalist and capitalist compromises—on behalf of conquest and slavery—"were never the only legacies on offer." They "don't negate the radical claim on what else happened" and "what else was dreamed." Those dreams are ahead of us. **BR**

The entrance to a bunker at the factory of Atlas Survival Shelters in Sulphur Springs, Texas.
Image: Getty Images

A YEAR OF MAGICAL THINKING

Olúfẹ́mi O. Táíwò

ON THE NIGHT of April 25, a lone gunman attacked the White House Correspondents' Dinner, sending off the predictable wave of condemnations of political violence by U.S. public officials, from federal legislators to state officials. As Michigan Senator Elissa Slotkin put it, "Political violence has no place in America." But there seems to be plenty of room for violence of the apparently nonpolitical sort: federal immigration agencies have used the recent push for mass deportations to accelerate their long and violent history with high-profile murders on the street and in their detention centers; as of April 23, the U.S. military has killed at least 186 people in a consistent campaign of bombings in Latin American waters; and there were 121 mass shootings in the first 112 days of the year, making mass shootings of the kind attempted at the Correspondents' Dinner a statistically daily occurrence. Public officials are appalled, then, to live in the same world as the rest of us.

The structure whose supports our elites are steadily kicking down is also the one that props up their own personal safety.

The elite's presumed exemption from violence rests on a broader bedrock of delusion that exists in its most virulent form on the ascendant American right. Last summer, U.S. Representative Madeleine Dean wielded the most unlikely of rhetorical weapons in a debate on the congressional floor: a banana. Across her sat Commerce Secretary Howard Lutnick, attempting to defend the Trump administration's tariff policy. After confirming with Lutnick that the president's baseline 10 percent tariff applied to banana imports, Dean explained that the price of bananas at Walmart had risen 8 percent. To which Lutnick replied: "If you build in America, there is no tariff." This exchange did not exactly soar to the heights of the historic Lincoln-Douglas debates, but it was no less illuminating of the basic political conundrum of our era: a critical mass of the political leadership of the United States appears to sincerely believe in magic.

What few banana plantations operate in the United States produce some 3,600 tons of bananas—a rounding error by comparison to the production from Guatemala, which produces 2.8 million tons a year. Plus, the fact that one cannot effectively "build" this tropical fruit at scale in the United States is intimately related to some fairly important facts about twentieth-century U.S. politics, including a four-decade stretch of wars and military interventions and a CIA-backed coup that inaugurated four decades of genocide in the very country that now provides us with the lion's share of our bananas.

It would be easy to handwave this away as a one-off slip-up or lapse in message discipline. But the blasé attitude of the ruling class toward the Banana Question fits squarely into a pattern being set across an ever-expanding list of topics. The present administration has scaled back environmental protections against toxic chemicals and dismantled climate rules and subsidies, eliminated vaccine recommendations for children while cutting funding for food safety inspections, and slashed the budget of the office that collects tax revenue while claiming its other layoffs were motivated by a concern over government debt. And it has done all of this while initiating a war in the most politically volatile region of the world on the flimsiest of pretexts, causing disastrous knock-on effects that are already sending energy markets into tumult and threatening to spur a global crisis in food production.

No doubt, Lutnick was bullshitting, and he was bullshitting because he understands himself to live in a world constrained only by the whims and attention span of his boss, rather than the basic contours of reality that the rest of us navigate by way of quaint norms of truthfulness and honesty. The Trump administration sustains this carelessness by holding onto a raft of genuine insight amid the sea of delusion: it has, up until now, been extraordinarily successful in making other people pay the price for its mistakes and crimes. But that raft is thin. The structure whose supports our elites are steadily kicking down is also the one that props up their own personal safety from disaster and political invulnerability to accountability. And all of this can go away.

IT IS EASIEST to make the case that all of this can go away by reflecting on the fact that it has. The COVID-19 pandemic remains with us in 2026, suppressed only by historic and ongoing efforts from researchers and medical professionals. Some people took health precautions less seriously in response to information that poor people of color were more severely affected by the virus than other groups. But "safer" does not mean safe: by one statistical analysis, the poorest and richest counties in the United States contracted COVID-19 at similar rates, though residents of richer counties were likelier to survive the ordeal. Past epidemics and public health crises from polio to the Spanish flu follow this same broad pattern: while unsurprisingly, the poor and socially marginalized are hit first and worst, any delusions of invulnerability harbored by the rich are soon punished. As public health researcher Svenn-Erik Mamelund puts it, "The first wave hits the poor, the second wave hits the rich." The recent historic rise in measles infection levels, closely following the Trump administration's stoking of anti-vax sentiment, suggests that the relevance of these little history lessons is already more than academic.

But communicable diseases are only one way to pierce the delusions of the rich that the ills of the social order are someone else's problem. Historian Rachel G. Hoffman described the political culture that evolved at the end of the nineteenth century as an "age of assassination" in which political protesters "tried to kill nearly every major European ruler and head of state." The closure of that age was not inevitable. It came about due to specific political interventions and historical developments—including the collapse of the French monarchy and the development of comprehensive labor law in the United States—that undermined the perceived legitimacy of politics done by these particular means. In other words, the resulting order has been less the outcome of an irreversible law of human progress than a détente produced by steel and blood.

Today, political violence looks to be on the rise again, from the most recent attempt on Trump's life to the murders of state legislators in Minnesota, the broad-daylight assassination of a health care executive, and the firebombing of the home of tech mogul Sam Altman. Commentators horrified by the popularity of Luigi Mangione would be wise to reflect on the fact that, in the years Hoffman studied, the utility of assassinations and terrorism was openly advocated for by political groups, whether by the French Jacobins, the Russian narodniks, or the U.S. anarchists avowing the "propaganda of the deed," all of which enjoyed a level of political support and sympathy above that of fringe outsiders. The current trend, which includes the outpouring of open sympathy for Mangione as well as a follow-up attack on Altman's house, suggests that the norm against open advocacy for political violence is not only reversible but has perhaps already been reversed—the logical consequence of undermined trust across all social institutions, among them the "legitimate" formal systems one might hope would displace violence as an outlet for expressing and resolving political disagreements.

On some level, they know. How else can we interpret U.S. corporate and political elites' chatter about "colonizing Mars" except as an admission that the present course of politics doomed the planet? But the raft of insight is thin indeed, and the seas of delusion stormy. Rather than bringing their considerable economic control and political influence to bear on addressing the ecological collapse of the planet, scores of the hyperrich are instead adding another layer of delusion: the apocalypse bunker. Meanwhile, the President immediately pivoted from the third public attempt on his life to shilling for his "Militarily Secure Top Secret Ballroom," which, as he assured the press, would have bulletproof glass and a drone-proof structure. Those in power may pretend not to know where the present political trajectories are taking us, but they seem to sense that they'll have to hide. In short, we are ruled by a class of people who seem either to believe or presume that war, disease, and apocalyptic destruction are things that will only ever happen to poorer and browner people. There's essentially no other way to explain why the Trump administration is so eagerly destroying so much that does, in fact, protect wealthier and whiter Americans.

Those in power may pretend not to know where the present political trajectories are taking us, but they sense that they'll have to hide.

Of course, it is simply not true—and we are clearly in an era where this needs to be said outright—that war, disease, and apocalyptic destruction can be contained to only affect poorer and browner people. Neither wealth nor social privilege can fully eliminate the risk of infectious disease, reverse the direction of a hurricane approaching landfall, or hold back the waters from entering the floodplain, whatever relative advantage it may confer in getting the nice spots of the rubble, or the finest bunker to live out one's days in hiding. Of course, debunking the delusion won't solve our political problems: we should not expect enough of these people to ever appreciate reality—at least, not via mere fact-checking. But we cannot afford to continue feeding the delusions. Before the Epstein files were slow-walked in the media, the architects of the 2008 financial crisis were almost exclusively bailed out rather than jailed, while those who orchestrated the invasion of Iraq have faced no legal or criminal repercussions at all, like those complicit, more recently, in the genocidal campaign in Gaza. It is this—the load-bearing, incontrovertible reality of elite impunity—that serves as their flimsy tether to the real world underneath the bluster and fantasy.

If we wait for the hyperrich to finally realize that their fates are tied to ours—for their children to contract measles, or for them to get cabin fever in their apocalypse bunkers—it will be too late for many of the rest of us. A better, quicker path out of this situation? Proving to the plutocrats that they actually are in the same game and bound by the same rules as common people by enacting harsh civil, criminal, and social penalties on those who have orchestrated our present political moment. This can be done within the confines of the rule of law—but only if legal consequences are swift, painful, and delivered on a timescale they cannot ignore. Minnesota prosecutors' recent charging of ICE officials for crimes is one step forward in the process of presenting the administration with consequences it cannot fantasize away. But it will take scores more of these thrusts, aimed at officials far higher up the political food chain, to pierce the veil of invulnerability currently launching warships toward the Strait of Hormuz. We are going to have to make war their problem. **BR**

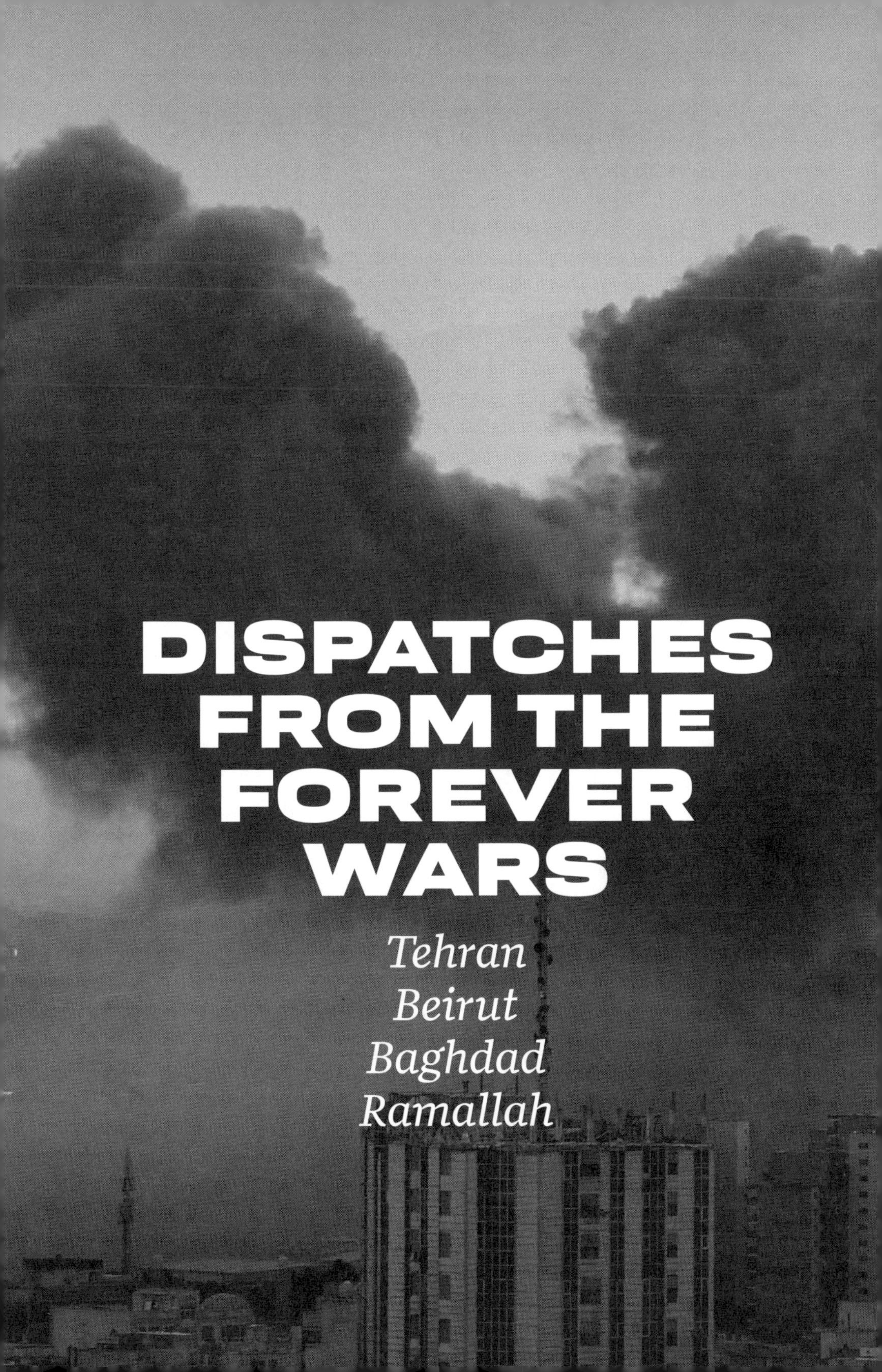

DISPATCHES FROM THE FOREVER WARS

Tehran
Beirut
Baghdad
Ramallah

THE CATASTROPHE THAT HAS BEFALLEN ALL OF US

translated by Naghmeh Sohrabi

When the U.S.-Israeli war on Iran started on February 28, I didn't hear from my oldest friend, an educator who runs an art center in Tehran, for eight long days. Rahaa, as I'll call her here, is in her fifties. We both lived through the bombardment of Tehran during the Iran-Iraq war from 1980 to 1988. After living through last year's twelve-day war, she is now living through bombardment again.

When Rahaa finally called me on March 8, she was overcome with anxiety. I invited her to keep a war diary, in part as a way to cope; she told me she would think about it. When she managed to break through the Islamic Republic's internet blackout a week ago, she sent pages of text. What follows is my abbreviated translation of her reflections on "the catastrophe that has befallen all of us." It is published here with her permission.

25 Esfand 1404 [March 16, 2026]

BBC PERSIAN IS BROADCASTING Trump speaking. He is talking about war with Iran. I really dislike him. I disliked him since his first presidency. He reminds me of [former Iranian president Mahmoud] Ahmadinejad. Vulgar and pretentious. I took a mild painkiller and muted the TV to write.

On Saturday I went to Ekbatan to pick up Mom to take her to the doctor. An endocrinologist. The doctor's office turned out to be in front of a Basij checkpoint. I wasn't expecting that. I pulled over right behind the Basij vehicle at the checkpoint to let my mom out. As I pressed the brakes to stop, one of the boys, very young, with a pleasant face and stylish glasses, whose face looked more like that of an anti-Basij youth, and yet he wore Basij-military clothes and had a weapon, came forward and said hello, please don't stop here. I said hello, I'm dropping my mom off and leaving, I'm not parking. With a smile and good manners he said it's no problem for you to park here, but if they hit us your car might get damaged. . . .

Suddenly I was confused. I couldn't believe what I heard. It was as if in a brief moment our relationship changed. I said God forbid. I don't know if he understood that I meant, *God forbid they hit you*. He said let me help get your mother out. I said no, I'll get her out. But he was already on the other side of the car, helping Mom get out with great care and kindness. And I just kept thanking him. There was neither anger nor fear between us; there was empathy and respect and very polite social interaction, and of course my heart was breaking from sorrow.

I said to the boy at the checkpoint, God forbid. I don't know if he understood that I meant, *God forbid the drone hit you.*

Mom got out, I thanked the boy a lot and drove forward, and while escaping that situation I was thinking whether it was right to park much farther away from them. Are we different? Do I have the right to distance myself from a dangerous situation because of the presence of those few young boys who are the targets of Israeli drones? I thought about that boy leaving home in the morning to come to the checkpoint: How did he say goodbye to his family? Did he say *Mom, cook pasta for lunch*? Or maybe he is fasting and asked for something sweet for iftar? Or did he say *Mom, if I am martyred forgive me*? Or phrases like that used by Basijis who still think there is martyrdom and elevation and ascension?

While intermittently crying I went farther up the road then turned around and parked on the other side. I was sure that if there were a drone attack, I was still too close for it to matter, but I had no choice. I had to get to Mom quickly, who was going up the stairs of the doctor's building. Sorrow was overwhelming me. I got out and when I was out of the Basijis' line of sight, I burst into tears.

I know the Basij are hated by so many people. I know people are angry, hurt, still grieving for the brutality with which so many people were killed just two months ago. I feel the same but still I wanted to go up to the young boy and say: my boy, go home, tell all of them to go home. Your lives are precious. Even though all of us people, after all these years, are angry, even though now we're pouring all our anger onto you and those like you, your lives are precious too. Don't you have a mother? Don't you have someone waiting for you? Aren't you a child of Iran? War is an asset to the powerful, so why should you, just a young boy, pay its debts?

If I told this to anyone around me, I could hear in my head that they'd call me a supporter of the Islamic Republic. To feel sadness at the death of this kid and so many kids like him now brands you as a regime supporter. When all it is is just grief for the catastrophe that has befallen all of us.

Mom's doctor didn't show up so we left. I told Mom come quickly, very quickly. She said why? I said it's dangerous here. She said I can't. I said even if you can't, you have to walk fast, and I pulled her along as much as I could. Then her eye caught the produce market and she said shall we shop? There was no way to say no. I thought well if I die, at least I'm with my mother, at least my mother won't feel the loss of a child, and I said okay let's go. At the entrance she sat on a chair and I rushed to quickly get what she wanted from various stalls when I noticed a juice shop among them. I got two carrot orange juices and in that awful and ugly produce market, amid the wave of general anxiety, with a bag of eggplants and carrots in hand, we drank juice and it felt very good, as if we weren't in the middle of war. I also acted carefree and let that mother-daughter joy continue between us. In the end it's just death; that's not something strange, seize the moment!

We went home and through a call with a friend I managed to buy a VPN and connect. Oh my God! Two weeks without internet was terrible.

As I write this, next to me is a bag of mixed nuts that when the war started I ordered from somewhere other than my usual store, whose quality is way better than these. But I now try to shop from businesses that aren't doing well to help them from going under. So many small shops are suffering and it's painful. After dropping Mom at home I went wandering around and buying small things. There is a girl who used to be a street vendor and for about two years now has opened her own shop; I went and bought two pairs of underwear and a pair of tights from her. I didn't need any of them, but I thought it is our duty to help each other.

The landlord has messaged me and increased the rent by 30 percent for next year, though because of the war I might lose about 40 percent of my monthly income; I have to increase the rent, which is 30 percent of my income, by 30 percent.

On Saturday evening I got Mom to get up and we went to Café Anseh. To those same three girls who are very lovely. We entered and I said "hello friends of wartime!" In the previous war too, on a day when I had been devastated, I went there and drank coffee and felt better. We stayed about half an hour and then came out to go buy trash bags and toilet paper when the sound of anti-aircraft systems, these days called air defense, started. We said forget it, let's go home, and returned home. I brought my overnight bag from my car and stayed at Mom's house that night. At the end of the night each of us watched a silly Turkish series we follow in turn—first Mom, then me—and then we went to sleep.

Well, I didn't fall asleep. I don't remember whether there was an attack or not, but I didn't sleep until five in the morning when I finally fell asleep on the couch, and near 9 a.m. I saw Mom sitting at the dining table about to eat breakfast. She had waited, but I hadn't woken up. I ate breakfast with tea and no coffee and got ready very quickly, like a dog in hell, to come home. Mom took a shower and I blow-dried her hair. She is very worried about why I haven't gone to the hairdresser yet for Nowruz [Persian New Year on March 20]. I told her I don't enter unfamiliar buildings these days. She said are you going to a new hairdresser? I said no, but I don't go to even slightly unfamiliar places these days. I didn't tell her that I don't even feel like going to the hairdresser; I don't want my hair to be made up. Although I put on makeup three times a day and wear nice clothes, I don't want to go to the hairdresser.

At six in the morning the next day I looked at my phone and saw Ali had written: give some news about yourself. And the next message: I'm very worried. I wrote: what?! why?! last night was very calm.

Then I went and checked the online news and I saw they had hit Tehran so much it had become a sieve. I looked around my bed and felt that I should by all counts be standing among the ruins of my house. But no. Around me was intact. I laughed. I thought poor Ali must have thought, *I was so foolish worrying for nothing*. Honestly I was very happy that I had slept until morning and hadn't felt a thing. Lately there has been almost no night that I have slept so completely detached from the world.

I don't know at which level of Maslow's hierarchy I am stuck, but I know I am not at the level where cultural needs should be addressed. These days I haven't read literature at all. I haven't even thought about it. I almost constantly have a headache and a heavy feeling on my heart and constant irritable bowel syndrome. During every attack I get stuck between taking shelter and squeezing into the toilet.

The image of the Basij boy helping my mother out of the car doesn't leave my mind.

I don't understand cheering on the war. I don't understand being happy about Iran burning. My heart bleeds for people dying. They hit the Javadiyeh neighborhood in south Tehran; many houses in that worn-out, old, and poor area were destroyed. A family of six all died under the rubble. And countless others whose news has not been recorded anywhere.

War belongs to innocent people.

When I was returning from Mom's house, on the other side of the street another group of Basijis had blocked the street for a checkpoint. In my heart hatred and anger toward them surged again, and at the same time sorrow and grief that they might lose their lives any minute. This push and pull, this fury at the regime and sorrow at the futility of war, this anger at boys playing men at checkpoints and the sadness that these children of Iran could die in a drone attack, brought me to tears.

This evening I went out for a drive. The sun was setting and darkness was beginning to descend. Night had not yet swallowed the destroyed FARAJA building [Iran's law enforcement headquarters] and its twisted railings and the torn billboards along the highway. A darkness darker than night keeps the taste of war more persistent under the tongue and among the folds of the brain and between the right and left atrium of the heart and inside the inflamed intestines.

I got home and again images of war kept playing before my eyes. It is a quarter to twelve at night and the air defense has become active again. **BR**

MILLENARIAN FANTASIES

Joelle M. Abi-Rached

March 11, 2026

In Beirut, we start our days with the latest litany of places and people hit overnight, a deluge of stories and images: buildings targeted, cars struck on highways, families wiped out. Evacuation orders drop at 11 p.m., then midnight, 1 a.m., 2 a.m., 3 a.m., 4 a.m., 5 a.m., 6 a.m.—then the bombing follows and the cycle starts again: more displaced families, more anger in the streets, more despair. The toll has now risen to more than 500 killed (including more than 80 children), more than 700,000 displaced, and more than 1,400 wounded. I am reminded of Cavafy's "Waiting for the Barbarians," though the kind of waiting his poem evokes now seems almost quaint: in Lebanon, the barbarians are no longer expected at the gates but have seeped into the very atmosphere of a disordered world. Here, violence is not a singular event but something in the air one inhales, gradually learning to domesticate and contain.

By March 3, a few days after the United States launched Operation Epic Fury, the Israeli military had issued evacuation orders affecting more than 100 villages and towns in southern Lebanon (an area two and a half times the size of New York City), as well as parts of the Beqaa Valley, while also approving further advances inside Lebanese territory, all in the name of prevention and self-defense. Human Rights Watch warns these sweeping orders raise "serious risks of violations of the laws of war"—but who's listening? Israel's specious logic is the same as that voiced by Marco Rubio, who claimed Washington struck Iran first because it expected an Israeli attack to trigger Iranian retaliation against U.S. forces. Preventive war is not, in itself, a settled legal justification under international law, and yet few are seriously contesting it. Apart from Spain and a few other dissenting voices, too many European leaders remain timid, unwilling to confront either Trump or Israel.

Surrounding all this is a broader collective delusion couched in the language of apocalyptic politics, where religion is weaponized to sanctify war. Christian Zionist pastors recently gathered in the Oval Office to bless the president in a surreal spectacle of ideological fervor and denial. (Imagine if any other nation—besides Israel, that is—displayed such behavior.) War as prophecy, devastation as fulfillment, catastrophe as a necessary prelude to the Second Coming; the Third Temple rebuilt, history consumed by apocalyptic fantasy, and humanity somehow redeemed afterward. Absurd as it sounds, this is reportedly what some U.S. military personnel were told they were doing in Iran: waging a holy war to hasten the return of Christ. In any other context, this would be recognized as dangerous fanaticism, the mirror image of holy jihad, if not a symptom of a psychiatric condition. Yet this is no longer fringe rhetoric.

A Beirut building destroyed in an Israeli air raid. Image: AP Images

In Beirut, the "most moral army in the world," as the IDF likes to call itself, appears, so far, to have practiced some restraint: the thousands living in targeted areas are issued orders and given neatly mapped-out routes by which to flee, all under the ceaseless buzz of drones—the strikes guided by AI-powered technology that feeds, in turn, on the personal reflections, data, and communications we have unknowingly surrendered. The banality of evil has been inscribed into an algorithm.

The Israeli army seems restless, and increasingly innovative, deploying terror alongside a campaign of fear.

On March 6, we received a warning that the next bombing, set to flatten a chunk of Beirut's southern suburbs, an area the size of lower Manhattan, might damage many more buildings across the city, too. Since we do not have bomb shelters, and since remaining indoors did not feel right—I have bad memories of spending nights in shaking buildings under bombardment, an experience I would not recommend—we chose instead to wait on the soccer field of the American University of Beirut, an area near the campus where displaced families have clustered.

The IDF seems less restrained when it comes to Sidon, Tyre, the south, and the Beqaa—biblical cities and territories whose soil one might have expected them to regard with some respect. In a surreal operation on March 7, Israeli helicopters dropped troops in Nabi Chit, a town named after the Prophet Seth (the son of Adam), to recover the remains of Ron Arad, an Israeli Air Force navigator who has been missing since 1986, when his plane went down over Lebanon. The fate of Arad, captured by the Amal movement and later believed to have been transferred to Hezbollah, has remained unknown for decades and has become one of Israel's most enduring military obsessions. That night, the air and ground raids left at least forty dead, including Lebanese soldiers, and inflicted apocalyptic damage to the town.

In recent days, Beirut's Corniche has filled with refugees and displaced families, the poorest sleeping in their cars or in makeshift tents nearby, the better-off finding whatever hotel rooms they can. At around 3 a.m. on March 8, a hotel in the seaside neighborhood of Raouché, famous for its views of the iconic Pigeon Rocks just off the coast, was hit in an IDF drone strike, killing at least four people and wounding ten. According to Israel, the four people targeted in the corner suite on the fourth floor were allegedly Iran-linked individuals planning an operation.

IN THE WAKE of the genocidal onslaught on Gaza, Lebanon is once again being drawn into a familiar cycle: abandonment, impunity, and the normalization of violence as the language of international law and human rights is hollowed out in real time. Has anything changed? Yes—and yet, not much. Hezbollah is markedly diminished; some displaced families are even angry with it. Israel's army seems to be following the same logic it deployed—or rather perfected—in Gaza: emptying out entire areas through what amounts, in effect, to ethnic cleansing, used both as military tactic and psychological warfare against the population. The displaced then move to other parts of Lebanon, which in turn become potential targets, fueling local resentment and intensifying public anger toward Hezbollah.

Lebanon is once again being drawn into a familiar cycle: abandonment, impunity, and the normalization of violence.

The Lebanese army has managed to deploy south of the Litani River—the area Israel wants to demilitarize and effectively cleanse of Hezbollah's presence—and has confiscated some of the group's weapons caches there. But it remains weakened, overstretched, and poorly paid; it is clearly not in a position to fully disarm Hezbollah, a party that has entrenched itself militarily and politically since Israel's invasion of Lebanon in 1982. In the past, the Lebanese army, wary of provoking civil strife, has been reluctant to confront Hezbollah directly. But the new government, formed last February under prime minister Nawaf Salam after president Joseph Aoun's election, has given the army greater political cover to curb what the state now considers as Hezbollah's unauthorized military activity. In a historic step, the government has moved to ban its military operations and to reinforce the principle that arms should be held exclusively by the state.

Nevertheless, pockets of Hezbollah remain, especially beyond the areas where the army has expanded its presence. The organization appears more closely tied than before to Iranian strategic calculations and to the Islamic Revolutionary Guard Corps. At the same time, Hezbollah and its supporters continue to frame their role as being part of Lebanon's defense against Israel. Since the cessation of hostilities took effect in November 2024, the United Nations Interim Force in Lebanon and others have documented thousands of Israeli air and ground violations north of the Blue Line, while Hezbollah's own military activity has been far more limited. In that context, it would be premature to describe the group as simply "disloyal" to its Shiite base, especially if Israel ends up occupying part of the country.

What exactly will the latest round of Israeli bombings set in motion? After years during which Hezbollah and its allies in power hollowed out the Lebanese state's capacity to act, this may mark the dramatic end of an era that began with the Iranian Islamic Revolution of 1979—or simply usher in a new era of chaos or renewed enmity.

I have often wondered what it means to be a witness in a place where empires have treated the landscape as a ledger, arriving, departing, returning, and always leaving behind a record of their passage. Just north of Beirut is Nahr el-Kalb—Arabic for "Dog River," or *Lyco Flumen* as it was known to the Romans. Along the cliffside pass above it, armies and rulers have for centuries carved stelae and inscriptions to mark campaigns, roadworks, occupations, and political events, forming an unusually dense in situ archive that stretches from Pharaonic Egypt through Neo-Assyrian and Neo-Babylonian rulers, into the Greco-Roman periods, and then into the modern era. To stand at Nahr el-Kalb is to confront the old fantasy that violence can somehow be made decipherable once it is inscribed; that domination becomes historical, and therefore settled, once recorded in stone. But stone does not settle anything. It only shows that the impulse to mark, to announce *We were here*, has always accompanied the impulse to destroy. This archive does not console, teach, or redeem. It simply accumulates as generations of traumatized populations endure and persevere.

Today, as empires rise and wane around us, we seem to be living through a similar moment. Lebanon is caught between two narrow theocratic projects: that of Iran and that of Israel. Yet however unsustainable and self-destructive each may be, only the latter possesses the power to turn its designs into reality, backed by the military might of the American Empire. What we are witnessing, then, is the renewal of a nakedly imperial project: a politics of permanent siege, existential paranoia, and millenarian last stands.

The war with Iran also looks like a convenient distraction from the accelerating dispossession of Palestinians in the occupied West Bank and the catastrophic situation in Gaza. Israel's strategy is by now familiar: strike, ethnically cleanse, move, and expand. Its incursions into southern Lebanon and even Syria look less like a new doctrine than the revival of an older strategic vision associated with Ben-Gurion: preemption, cross-border force, and the reshaping of neighboring realities through military power. Whatever form this strategy takes, Palestine will remain the region's deepest and most enduring wound.

Our hospital at the American University of Beirut is preparing for an imminent disaster, including chemical, biological, radiological, and nuclear scenarios. In my classes I teach these very histories, along with their devastating implications for ethics, bodies, and minds. Never did I imagine that one day, I would be living through them myself. What happens next is hard to predict. Yet again, the lived and felt and lasting certainty is damage and destruction, wrought by fantasies of unchecked domination that play out as if the long nineteenth century never ended. **BR**

THE SHADOW OF IRAQ

Nabil Salih

March 10, 2026

ON MARCH 4, amid the ebb and flow of Baghdad's infamous traffic, I saw a forty-something peddler sporting a bunny headband that glowed in the dark as he walked the neck of Al-Sinak bridge, hawking toys he carried in both hands. To his left was the Al-Mansour Melia, a derelict hotel built in the early 1980s where CIA operatives once checked in to offer their Iraqi counterparts satellite maps during Iraq's war against the Ayatollah. To his right was a security complex with a pile of concrete security barriers waiting to be deployed in future protests. And behind him was Tehran's embassy. On its mammoth T-walls were plastered the faces of some of those who perished in the twelve-day war against the Islamic Republic last year. A sign called them "victims of the Zionist aggression." Among them was a little girl whose eyes stared into the void, a mute emissary from the afterlife who can no longer play.

At the other end of the bridge, the downtown's atrophied architectural splendor dissolved into the night. On the fifth day of the unprovoked U.S.-Israeli war on Iran, the national power grid was down due to gas shortages. The heart of the city was "quiet as a graveyard," as the late Charles Simic once wrote. Driving to the east bank, I sped over the shallow waters of the Tigris and headed toward a protest just outside the Green Zone. For days, angry youths had gathered in a standoff with security forces, who prevented them from reaching Washington's embassy. Policemen stood sentinel at hastily erected roadblocks—as locals call them, flying checkpoints—just as they did after 2003, when Saddam Hussein's statue last stood at Al-Firdous Square. Nearly twenty-three years to the day after I watched its toppling on TV from a village outside Baghdad, I was greeted by a giant billboard looming over the entrance of the nearby Al-Alwiyah Club, where Gertrude Bell had lounged. It showed the image of Ali Khamenei, whose assassination has crowned him in the halo of martyrdom.

Down the street a child sold water outside the French Embassy ghetto. The guarded enclave houses international press bureaus where would-be "Middle East" editors had built easy careers at a time when the War on Terror presented hundreds of corpses a day. I parked on a side street in Al-Karrada and got on a bus headed to the demonstration near the hanging 14th of July Bridge. Known as Al-Jisr al-Mu'allaq, it was designed by David B. Steinman and was later bombed during the Gulf War in 1991. More than 85,000 tons of explosives destroyed everything from baby milk factories to civilian shelters. Like broken sentences, several bridges fell in the Tigris, failing to touch the other shore. Now the 14th of July was the sole border keeping an angry mass from reaching the fortified embassy, a sprawling compound on an exclusive highway inaccessible to locals.

By nightfall, some two hundred had gathered under an overpass that is yet to open to traffic. The construction is one of many plans inaugurated by Prime Minister Mohammed al-Sudani, whose schizophrenic remodeling of Baghdad intends to project prosperity but has only erected an unconvincing simulacrum. Al-Sudani, who seems keen on preventing an escalation, ordering the arrest of those firing rockets at U.S. forces and energy facilities, was the target of scurrilous chants throughout the night, insulted and heckled as "an American agent." One protester waved the Iranian flag; others hoisted portraits of Khamenei and Sayyid Muhammad Sadiq al-Sadr (father of prominent Shia cleric Muqtada al-Sadr), himself assassinated in 1999. One image showed Ayatollah Sayyid Ali al-Sistani, whose statement from earlier in the day condemned the U.S.-Israeli aggression and called for "a just and peaceful resolution to [the crisis posed by] Iran's nuclear program."

Shiism and the ready-made category of "proxies" are too simplistic explanations for these protests and expressions of cathartic anger.

The atmosphere was tense but the standoff was peaceful, unlike previous nights when, according to security forces, "a number of security members came under fire and had their caravans and one of their vehicles burned." Riot police had fired tear gas in return, dispersing the crowd. A few young women in their black abayas had showed up—a palpable legacy of the 2019 October Uprising, which saw thousands of young people turn out to protest government corruption, foreign intervention, low wages, and poor public services—but when I visited, the crowd mostly comprised middle-aged and young men. They sat on the curb or milled about, following the latest news on Telegram. It was a mournful and modest congregation, punctuated by chants against "the great Satan" that is the United States. Earlier in the evening news had come from Babil province, where a leader of Katai'b Hezbollah, a paramilitary group, was assassinated. His casket would be taken to his home in Baghdad the next morning for a final goodbye. Footage showed a modest dwelling in a blue-collar neighborhood, very different from the former bourgeois avenues favored by the nouveaux riches after 2003, including Sunnis and the self-styled revolutionary Shia elite.

Not everyone under the overpass that night was a member of Al-Hashd al-Shaabi, or the Popular Mobilization Units, the constellation of paramilitary groups that fought the Islamic State before some factions metamorphosed into considerable political and economic entities. Someone in his early twenties asked if it was safe for him to wade deep into the crowd. I told him it seemed fine, but he should be alert. It seemed to be his first protest. He reminded me of two young men I had met during the 2019 protests who had lost brothers fighting against the caliphate only to be forgotten, with not even a pension to support the families they left behind. Had he lost a brother in Mosul? I kept the thought to myself as he walked away. The words "Death to America" were graffitied in red paint on pillars near where we stood.

Shiism and the ready-made category of "proxies" are too simplistic explanations for these protests and expressions of cathartic anger. Something afoul persists. The roads taken by each protester are riddled with traumatic memories from years of occupation. Iraq remains a country with deep wounds of neocolonialism and camouflaged ruination. Its unions and revolutionary parties have long lost their capacity to mobilize. For some of those living in liminal districts, the response seems less about the attack on the Islamic Republic itself; rather, the sight of another Muslim of humble origins murdered for standing up to common enemies during a holy month and amid genocide in Gaza is unbearable, to say nothing of the humiliation caused by another defeat before Israel. Palestine and Dahiyeh are not so easily forgotten, no matter the American codger's "Board of Peace" and his spurious declaration that the war on the besieged strip is over. The weight of all the concrete in Gaza is crushing, the images from the elementary school bombed in Minab impossible to unsee. In personalizing Khamenei's loss some find an antidote against what depersonalizes and makes life disposable and obsolete.

Yet the Shia are not a monolith; fissures run between the haves and have-nots as well as through the paramilitaries. In another demonstration last week, a young protester seemed livid that senior leaders ride in Tahoe SUVs to funeral halls but do not join them to help set the embassy alight, as they have done before. Comfortable with parliamentary representation, posts in the highest echelons of power, and access to state revenues and real estate investments, some Shia elites opt for restraint, even if factions under the moniker "Islamic Resistance in Iraq" carry out limited attacks against U.S. bases, mostly in Erbil. Their allies may be fighting an existential war that could also be theirs, but the status quo is unlikely to be traded for a coffin. Reactions have varied. Al-Sadr, at odds with Iran's allies inside Iraq, has been watching from the sidelines. Nouri al-Maliki, the former premier currently grooming himself for a third term, retracted his condolences for Khamenei on X and is making overtures to the Beltway. Sheikh Akram al-Ka'abi, leader of Harakat al-Nujaba', chastised his ilk for being "shaken and servile" before Donald Trump. His later invectives against the Shia political elite were scathing; in one he spoke of a rat "leaking information about the mujahideen to Cypriot and Jordanian intelligence."

By midnight, messaging from paramilitary leaders seemed to be taking a new dimension. One of them addressed U.S. citizens in their own tongue, urging them to "reclaim your country" and "protect your future." I drove away along Abu Nuwas, a riverine street named after an Abbasid poet known for his licentious verses and wine-soaked revelries. In one poem, he writes that he would only make the pilgrimage to Mecca "after Baghdad's delights expire." There were times when they seemed endless, but that night the riverside park that once housed Isma'il Fattah al-Turk's sculpture of the poet was silent, the grounds unkempt and strewn with litter. I thought of the specters of all those who could have walked the city streets but died too soon. The latest victim was Yanar Mohammed, a leftist women's rights activist murdered on March 2 outside her Baghdad residence by unidentified assassins. Her monochrome portrait, smiling, was plastered on the city's walls by her comrades at the Organization of Women's Freedom in Iraq. "We did this," the group stated in a message calling for protests on International Women's Day, "to say clearly that killing women will not stop women's struggle, and that bullets cannot silence the idea of freedom."

Against the risk of online vilification, some Iraqis, including Shia, express schadenfreude at the misfortune of their eastern neighbor, whose regime and its allies in Baghdad they blame for Iraq's decades of murder, displacement, and theft. In 2019, when unarmed youth took to the streets in a sect-transcendent uprising against the U.S.-installed regime and its neoliberal policies, the late supreme leader dismissed the movement as a Western plot. Hundreds were slain with impunity. But as plumes of smoke tower over Tehran, many recall the long nights when Baghdad was irreversibly defamiliarized by violence. I remembered the voice of the late communist poet Saadi Youssef. It was the United States, he writes in one poem, "that demolished a homeland over your head / and hired death squads / and uprooted the meaning of branches / from your garden."

In the days following March 4, the girl's image outside the Iranian embassy was replaced by Khamenei's. U.S.-Israeli raids on paramilitaries intensified, as have counterattacks. Oil fields, U.S. troops, hotels, and Kurdish Iranian opposition camps in Duhok, Erbil, and Suleimaniyah have been hit by drone and rocket attacks. On Telegram, Iranian-aligned armed factions claim over two dozen operations each day, with some hitting Basra and reaching as far as Kuwait and Jordan. The familiar wail of sirens has returned to the capital, and the U.S. embassy was targeted by rocket fire. Al-Sudani called it "a terrorist act." He insists Iraq shouldn't be forced into war, but a familiar miasma already pervades the air. This is a portrait of another nadir, on the other side of our "regime change." **BR**

AT THE GATES OF HELL

Raja Shehadeh

March 31, 2026

IT IS SPRING in Palestine, and Eid al-Fitr has just passed. It's customary to buy new clothes for the feast, but with people desperately short of funds, this tradition was out of reach for most this year. It was hard to find signs of celebration, even the smallest manifestations of joy, anywhere. In Ramallah, where I live, the city was quiet and subdued. Distress and worry were visible on people's faces. Since 2023, an already dire economic situation in the West Bank has been exacerbated by the Israeli government, which has withheld tax collected on behalf of the Palestinian Authority and prevented Palestinians from working in Israel. The long detours drivers must take to avoid a constantly expanding set of Israeli checkpoints have hiked up the price of local produce.

In another time, going for picnics in the lush green hills so full of wildflowers—anemones, cyclamen, and yellow mustard seed—would have been an affordable alternative to a grand feast. Yet this Eid, even that pleasure was denied. The hills around Ramallah are becoming more militarized by the day, with settler outposts being erected on high grounds and masked settlers brandishing machine guns roaming the area, ready to attack anyone daring to take a walk.

The Qalandia checkpoint in Ramallah on February 27. Image: Jaafar Ashtiyeh/AFP via Getty Images

On Saturday, March 21, an eighteen-year-old man from an illegal farming outpost called Shuva Yisrael Farms died in a traffic accident when his ATV collided with a car driven by a Palestinian. Without evidence that the Palestinian driver intended harm, settlers immediately took to social media to urge Israelis to carry out what one called "revenge and expulsion of the enemy." Their audience was eager to oblige, shooting and beating Palestinians and burning cars and homes in twenty-five near-simultaneous attacks in villages across the West Bank. Israel's defense minister, Bezalel Smotrich, extended condolences to the man's parents "over the murder of their son . . . who fell guarding our country while holding on to the land of Samaria." The deceased's father called his son a "communal sacrifice" for the settlement cause.

Not that the settlers have ever needed a reason to harass and beat Palestinians, destroy their property, and seize their farmland. Such violence has been ongoing since the early 1980s. At the time, under pressure from Israeli law professors, the Israeli attorney general appointed a committee of jurists to investigate law enforcement in the West Bank and Gaza. When the committee exposed numerous crimes carried out by Jewish settlers against Palestinians in the West Bank—assault, destruction of property, armed threats, shootings, and attacks on schoolchildren—settlers, as well as the police and army, tried to obstruct the publication of their findings. When they were finally released in 1984 in *The Karp Report: An Israeli Government Inquiry into Settler Violence Against Palestinians on the West Bank*, the government ignored it.

In addition to their decades of living under the threat of settler violence, Palestinians in the West Bank have long been accustomed to war's dangers. In Ramallah, where, like everywhere else in the West Bank, there are no bomb shelters, I have lived through seven wars—beginning with the Six-Day War of 1967—yet never have I felt so vulnerable as I do today. That isn't because of the Iranian and Hezbollah bombings: neither has targeted the West Bank, and only occasionally has shrapnel fallen here from missiles or interceptors (On March 18, for instance, an errant Iranian missile hit the town of Beit Awwa near Hebron, killing four women in a beauty salon and wounding thirteen others). It's because the war is being used as cover for a sharp rise in settler violence, with no apparent effort by Israel's government to control it.

UNTIL RECENTLY, the Israeli army was not an accomplice and the government did not overtly incite the settlers. Today, though, that has all changed: Israel's right wing, led by Itamar Ben-Gvir, Minister of National Security and a settler himself, unabashedly encourages the use of pogroms against villages spanning from the Jordan Valley to Israel's 1948 border—acts that constitute the ethnic cleansing of Palestinians. And armed settler militias, often operating with support from the army, attack and harass Palestinian communities across the West Bank in an effort to make life so unbearable for them that they will be forced out.

Since the latest war's onset, the settlers have become more emboldened than ever before. According to the Israeli monitoring group Yesh Din, there have been more than 257 reports of settler violence against Palestinians in the West Bank since the first U.S. airstrikes on Iran, including shootings, physical assaults, property damage, and threats. In this span, settlers have killed seven Palestinians, one of whom died after inhaling tear gas fired by Israeli soldiers amid a settler attack. In these attacks (and all the others over the decades in the West Bank), settlers take advantage of the approximately 898 military checkpoints and obstacles that severely restrict Palestinian mobility—permanent checkpoints, iron gates that close off villages, earth mounds, and roadblocks—knowing that, in the wake of their violence, ambulances will not be able to reach the victims in time.

West Bank Palestinians are determined to stay. If they face a new catastrophe, it will not be one of exile.

Israel has also authorized a construction push to build new settlements—an expansion effort that Smotrich, who grew up in the settlement of Beit El near Ramallah, has admitted is designed to bury the idea of a Palestinian state. Indeed, the construction has crept into areas of the West Bank that were supposed to be protected from it. Under the Oslo Accords of 1993-5, the West Bank was divided into three areas: Area C, comprising 60 percent of the land's area, is under full Israeli control; Area A, comprising 18 percent, is under the jurisdiction of the Palestinian Authority; Area B, the remainder, is under joint Israeli and Palestinian jurisdiction. Today, settlement does not stop at Area C, where settlers now outnumber Palestinians: it is now encroaching into Area B and even to Area A. Earlier this month, +972 Magazine reported that settlers have taken control of around 25,000 acres in the two Areas, bringing the total amount of land held by settler outposts across the West Bank to over 250,000 acres. And since the beginning of the year, the Israeli military has carried more frequent raids into Palestinian towns and cities in Area A to arrest residents, often without charge.

Compounding our constant pain at witnessing more and more of our land being colonized is the fact that Palestinians living in the West Bank cannot feel safe anywhere. On March 14, the Bani Odeh family were returning home to their village in Tammun after shopping in nearby

Nablus for Eid—a trip that requires passing through multiple checkpoints—when an undercover Israeli Border Police officer shot at their car, killing the father, mother, and two of their children. The Israeli Justice Ministry unit that probes police misconduct has yet to summon the murderers for questioning.

SOME HAVE CLAIMED that Palestinians are facing a second Nakba, the catastrophe of expulsion, but I am not so sure. In 1948-9, Palestinians were caught by surprise. They didn't fully realize what was happening and that they would never be allowed to return to the homes they were forced out of. Nor did they anticipate that the Zionists would deny that they ever constituted a national group with a long history tied to the land. At that time, so close to the Holocaust, the world sympathized with the Jewish plight, leading to an outpouring of support for the Zionists to establish a state of their own in Palestine.

These factors no longer exist—and in fact the opposite might be true. The destruction of Gaza has eroded international support for Israel. Neither Jordan nor Egypt is willing to participate in ethnic cleansing by receiving Palestinians forced out. And the Palestinian right to self-determination has won international recognition and support. Today, with the memory of the Nakba still so vivid, Palestinians are determined to stay. They will surely resist the effort by the settlers and the army to force them out en masse, yet with the war raging, the dangers they face have never been so great. If Palestinians in the West Bank face a new catastrophe, it will not be one of exile.

At home in Ramallah, I hear the sounds of the war—the explosions, the drones, the missiles and warplanes—and see images on television of buildings toppled, crumpled, crashing to the ground raising clouds of dust and debris, some burning, others falling in one large heap, the widescale destruction in Tel Aviv, Tehran, and Beirut. I shudder as I feel the shadow of Gaza's fate hanging over me. I'm surrounded by a looping reel of devastation in our cursed region. As we stand at the gates of Hell with no apparent route back, I wonder how much longer it will go on, this relentless, merciless, never-ending cycle. **BR**

IMPERIAL ANXIETIES

A roundtable discussion of the U.S.-Israeli war on Iran

Peyman Jafari, Ali Kadivar, Manijeh Moradian, Naghmeh Sohrabi, and Alex Shams

ON **MONDAY, APRIL 6,** Boston Review *convened a panel of distinguished scholars of Iranian politics, history, and culture to discuss the war on Iran initiated by the United States and Israel in late February. The following is an edited transcript of the event, moderated by Alex Shams. The panelists discuss the geopolitics of American and Israeli aggression, the long history of Western intervention in the region, reactions from within Iran and the Iranian diaspora, and the fate of struggles for freedom and democracy "under the boot of empire."*

ALEX SHAMS: More than 3,500 people have been killed in Iran since this unprovoked war of aggression began, in addition to nearly 1,500 people in Lebanon. All of us on this panel have loved ones in the region, and I just want to start by acknowledging that this is a very difficult time.

As with the Bush administration's invasion of Iraq in 2003, both Donald Trump and Benjamin Netanyahu have invoked vaguely preemptive rationales in response to unspecified "imminent" and "existential" threats from Iran, but this time the war propaganda has gotten far less buy-in than it did twenty years ago. Congress has not specifically authorized the use of force, as it did with the invasion of Iraq, and polls show that most Americans think the war should end and that it was wrong to use military force against Iran. We've seen both the United States and Israel give changing and inconsistent explanations of their goals, with no clarity about an endgame and apparent surprise that the Iranian government hasn't fallen. What's going on? How should we understand the aims and interests of the United States and Israel right now?

ALI KADIVAR: I think we have to start by zooming out and taking a longer view, seeing the current war as a part of a broader pattern in Iranian history—major wars in which Iran has been invaded, with serious consequences for Iran's political trajectory. Any Iranian living in the nineteenth or twentieth century, if they lived at least forty years, witnessed two major wars in their lifetime. I myself was born under the Iran-Iraq War; I have memories of bombs being dropped, missiles hitting cities, running into shelters. And by forcing the question of how to defend Iranian sovereignty, these wars have shaped political orders in Iran, crushing some and consolidating others.

The Constitutional Revolution that began in 1905 was one of these major projects. Under Mozaffar ad-Din Shah Qajar, Iran's response to territorial loss was to transform the political order by adopting a constitution, parliament, and rule of law—a nationalist and democratic response. But this order collapsed under external pressure in World War I, and then we see the rise of Reza Shah and the Pahlavi dynasty. This is a different political project: it modernizes constitutionalism, but puts aside parliament and the rule of law with the personalization of power. But this project also collapses during the Anglo-Soviet occupation of Iran in 1941. That prompts the rise of Mohammad Reza Shah Pahlavi, who is strengthened following the British- and American-backed coup of 1953 but eventually falls with the 1979 revolution. Then comes the Islamist project, which is religious and authoritarian but populist in the sense that it relies on mass mobilization, born in response to foreign intervention. The Iran-Iraq War helps this project to consolidate.

Now, with this U.S.-Israeli war of aggression, we are watching the pattern repeat. The Islamic Republic faces a situation similar to the 1980s: more militarized politics, hardline elites with a siege mentality, suppression of civil society, and increasing arrests and executions.

MANIJEH MORADIAN: To take it from a different angle, I think the United States and Israel have carried out genocide in Gaza, and they're seizing on this opportunity to try to assert control over the region through any amount of violence that they can get away with. They committed war crimes in Gaza, and they're committing war crimes in Iran. Carpet bombing cities is a war crime. Bombing civilian infrastructure is a war crime. Trump is obviously threatening to carry out even more war crimes, very brazenly and openly. The point is that the United States and Israel want to normalize this: they want the world to accept that this is the way it is, that they can get away with it, that they can do whatever they want. And the Iranian people are paying the price.

What makes this so challenging and devastating is that Iranian people are the targets of imperial war crimes and also ongoing systematic human rights violations by their own government. Iranians have been trying for a very long time to make change, and it's here that Ali's narrative of foreign intervention—how that has constrained and shaped different projects of resistance and state-making and society—is so important. Over the last several decades, we've seen, in one form or another, Iranians trying to make their society better, to make it less repressive, more equal, more livable. Protests, whether for reforms or for a different form of government altogether, have been met with intense state violence. Israel, the United States, and Iranian monarchists have swarmed like vultures to feed off of the despair, desperation, and helplessness that became widespread in Iran after the unprecedented scale of the crackdown on protesters in January.

"The United States and Israel want to normalize this. They want the world to accept that this is the way it is, that they can do whatever they want. The Iranian people are paying the price."

There's this word in Farsi, *estisal*, that is the word of the moment. It means despair. Despair can be mobilized to many different political ends, and unfortunately the most right-wing reactionary forces have been able to capitalize off and exploit it. People on the ground, having risen up over and over again, having been subjected to a massacre in January, are experiencing a moment of devastating defeat. Now they are being subjected to carpet bombing, the destruction of everything needed to live and to organize. At the same time, the Iranian government continues to hold thousands of political prisoners, to carry out executions of protesters, and to heavily surveil the population. I know I'm not alone in being very worried. It could get much worse if Trump makes good on his barbaric and maniacal threats.

Peyman Jafari: I think we have seen different rationales for this war exactly because making the real reason explicit would have been unhinged, even for Netanyahu and Trump. At the end of the day, from the Israeli perspective, it is really about eliminating any obstacle to its long-term project, which is the subjugation of the Palestinians. So this really starts in 1948 and continues through Israel's invasion of Egypt in 1956 with Britain and France, and then the 1967 and 1973 wars. This had nothing to do with political Islam, or Islamism: Israel was at war with secular Arab nationalism. And Netanyahu, of course, has subscribed to the Greater Israel plan.

As for the United States, Israel has always been an outpost of American empire in the Middle East. From the imperial point of view, the agency of ordinary people in the Middle East—whether Egyptians, Iranians, Iraqis—is a problem: they can be a danger when they rise up for democracy, for social equality, and against autocratic regimes. But maintaining one state totally dependent on American empire gives you some kind of assurance about power projection in the region. The war is therefore also about resurrecting, or entrenching, American empire. We Iranians tend to think it is all about us, but I think it has to do with the imperial anxieties of the American elite.

The messaging has thus been aimed not only at Iran—we will crush you, we will use enormous amounts of violence, we will send you back to the Stone Age—but also at Europeans, at U.S. allies: you will be disciplined. Two months ago, at a meeting in London, the Belgian prime minister said, "Being a happy vassal is one thing. Being an unhappy slave is something else entirely." The United States is making clear that this is the imperial hierarchy—the United States on top and then the Europeans. The war is also a signal to Russia and China that the United States is still the biggest military power. If its economic position has declined, the United States can compensate through sheer military might.

Naghmeh Sohrabi: I'll turn the question around and look at it from the other side—not the aims of the United States and Israel, but the aims of the Islamic Republic. Ali drew an important historical line, but I would say there are significant differences between this war and earlier moments. One concerns the way the war is being fought. This war is unlike the early years of the Iran-Iraq War, when the Iraqis had boots on the ground in Iranian territory and the Iranians were pushing the Iraqis back.

The current moment is much closer to the middle of that war, when it had become a war of attrition: Iran was continuing the war despite the fact that there were proposals to end it. And that's because, as Ali said, there are political projects connected to continuing this war. The primary objective of the Islamic Republic of Iran is the survival of the system.

Iran's response to the current war was entirely foreseeable. We have seen the Islamic Republic use the war to expand its own political projects, to make itself more stable and to continue to brutalize its own population. Something is lost if we simply characterize Iran's response as resistance, or self-defense. This is the system resisting. This is the system fighting. The country is being bombarded as we speak, literally right now; the Iranian government cannot and will not do anything to control that. What it is doing is lighting the region on fire in reaction to U.S. and Israeli aggression as a way to keep itself going. I think we need to keep that in mind when we're thinking about the various forces that have contributed to this moment.

SHAMS: Everyone on the panel today has at some point written about the distortions and misrepresentations of Iranian history and society in U.S. media and culture. I'd like us each to share an example along these lines that feels particularly relevant to understanding the current moment. If you could correct one major misunderstanding about Iran, what would it be?

JAFARI: The idea that this war was inevitable—that everything had to lead to this point because of Iran's domestic politics of authoritarianism and repression and its foreign politics of power projection in the region, its support for Bashar al-Assad in Syria and beyond. No doubt, these things are very problematic. But we have to understand that these policies did not emerge in a geopolitical and historical vacuum. International politics very much shaped these issues and foreclosed alternative paths and developments.

To give just one example, we still hugely underestimate the impact of the 2001 and 2003 invasions of Afghanistan and Iraq. At the time of these invasions, there was a vibrant reform project gaining ground in Iran, but the invasions helped conservatives undermine reform. The perception of a threat from outside aggressors—and the resulting militarization of

Iranian politics—foreclosed that development and made it much harder for Iranian civil society to fight back and organize.

So, we have to think about these moments where change was possible in terms of foreign policies. Western leaders often reduce the region's problems to Iran's role in the "axis of resistance." It's important to remember where that term comes from: it was coined as a foil to George W. Bush's "axis of evil" speech in 2002, when he named Iran alongside Iraq and North Korea as targets of the War on Terror. That speech, and the foreign policy that grew out of it, pushed Iran to closer alignment with Iraqi militias, Hezbollah, and other groups in order to consolidate that "axis of resistance." The point is that Iranians have been fighting for democracy on their own, and these foreign interventions have made that harder, not easier.

MORADIAN: There are so many misunderstandings. If I can only correct one, it would be the idea that the Islamic Republic is anti-imperialist, and that the only way to oppose imperialist war is therefore to support the Islamic Republic. This idea still circulates on the left in the United States and other parts of the world. I want to take it head on, since it feels like one of the many elephants in the room.

Iranians should obviously not be forced to choose between obliteration by the most powerful foreign militaries in the world and submission to a violent authoritarian state. Anti-imperialism as it has been practiced and preached by the Islamic Republic—as a tool for shoring up its power and crushing internal dissent—has done great damage by severing anti-imperialism from the ideas of freedom and justice that were once its animating force. I think we urgently need an alternative. In particular, we need a feminist approach to opposing genocide and war.

There's a widespread misconception that feminism is a Western invention, when in fact, different forms of feminist politics arise from lived experiences and material conditions of oppression all over the world. Yes, there can be right-wing, pro-war uses of feminism; we need to counter those with an anti-imperialist feminism of the kind that has emerged in Iran, Palestine, Iraq, and all over the Global South over the past several decades. This is not a new thing. Third World or Global South feminists have long had to theorize and organize at the intersection of postcolonial authoritarianism and the relentless pressures of imperialism.

In the context of Iran, only a feminist analysis, I think, can account for the ways that imperialist Western aggression through sanctions and war have exacerbated domestic repression, enriched a ruling oligarchy at the expense of everyone else, and justified violent crackdowns in the name of national security. Feminists have long explained that there's more than one source of oppression in the world, more than one form that bears down on people, their bodies and lives and futures, and that it's both possible and necessary to refuse all of the structures of militarism, patriarchy, and domination imposed from above. In short, anti-imperialism without feminism can easily collapse into support for authoritarianism, but feminism without anti-imperialism becomes cheerleading for empire. The record of Iranian history is very clear: there can be no freedom or democracy under the boot of empire.

"We still hugely underestimate the impact of the U.S. invasions of Afghanistan and Iraq. The perception of a threat from outside aggressors made it much harder for Iranian reformists to fight back and organize."

At the same time, we have to confront many Iranians' skepticism of anti-imperialism by clearing up the misconception that it means viewing the Iranian people as pawns in a geopolitical game, with no concern for their suffering at the hands of their own government and no solidarity with their aspirations for a more democratic society. But again, to do so, we need to reclaim anti-imperialism from the Islamic Republic and refashion it into a feminist antiwar framework. Anti-imperialism has to become bound to the preservation and defense of life against mass death, whoever is perpetrating it. And I think that was really the spirit of the Woman, Life, Freedom movement that emerged in Iran in 2022. One of my biggest concerns right now is to make sure that its legacy not be left to die under the rubble.

Sohrabi: For me, the biggest misunderstanding that has led to this moment is this undying idea that Iran is a totalitarian state, and that it has been the same for forty-seven years. Iran is not a totalitarian state;

it never has been. It's an authoritarian state, and those are very different things. What I mean is simply that the mainstream image in people's minds about Iran—the image that, for example, persists in the Western press and in the pro-war diaspora media—is that Iran is a top-down, consistently repressive state that wants to and can control every aspect of people's lives. But that has never been the reality of Iran. The population continues to claw open space for their own rights, to come up with new ideas. The Iranian intellectual scene is full of people—even at this moment, as the bombs are falling—who are trying to come up with ways to be in dialogue with each other and come up with new ideas to expand their rights for when the bombs stop falling.

This conceit of Iran's essential unchangingness is premised on the idea that as long as you have clerics in charge, or you have an Islamic Republic, or a theocracy, or whatever you want to call it, it's just more of the same, namely constant, top-down brutality. In fact, the Iranian political system has changed in important ways since 1979—from its first decade, under the Iran-Iraq War, to the period of reconstruction under President Hashemi Rafsanjani, which gave birth to the reform movement. According to every single measure, these changes have resulted in a different Iran—a different system of governance, a different economic system, a different role for the press, different ways that people interact with the state, different ways the state exercises violence on its population. Yet every time there was an election—and all of us were invited to comment as pundits in Western media—every response we got from the U.S. policy establishment was, *it makes no difference if people vote or not; this is not a free and fair electoral system, and the only context where votes matter is in a free and fair electoral system.*

That's not empirically true, but the idea never broke through the U.S. government discourse about the Islamic Republic. So we got to this point, three years after the Woman, Life, Freedom movement—which has radically changed what Iran looks like by getting rid of the veil as a visual marker of the country—when the Trump administration thought it could just get rid of Supreme Leader Ali Khamenei and somehow the same old unchanging system was just going to collapse as a result. It didn't, and it was never going to.

KADIVAR: A major misconception in foreign policy is that Iran is the biggest sponsor of terror in the world and the major source of instability in the region. It's not that the opposite is true—the Islamic Republic has indeed engaged in destabilizing acts; its support for Assad has been especially appalling, and in Iraq, the Iranian military fought with ISIS while terrorizing some Sunni communities. But Iran is not the only actor in the Middle East with dirty hands.

In reality, the biggest source of instability in the region is the United States. Its invasion of Iraq led to waves of wars and civil wars that still continue. Hundreds of thousands of Iraqis were killed in the ensuing violence, and ISIS emerged out of the power vacuum created by civil war. Close U.S. allies are other major sources of instability. The ongoing genocide against Palestinians committed by Israel—called the "only democracy in the region," with the "most moral army in the world"—is now expanding to Lebanon. The United Arab Emirates has its hands in the bloody civil war in Sudan; Saudi Arabia was bombing Yemen and starving Yemenis for a while a few years ago. Meanwhile, Turkey has supported Sunni extremist groups in Syria, where former fighter Ahmed al-Sharaa has become president. The issue is not that Iran has been a source of instability. The issue is that Iran has pursued a different regional order than the one desired by the United States. It's not necessarily a better order or worse order. Both orders have been authoritarian and exclusive, violent to those that are not defined to be included.

Another refrain is that Iran uses proxies, as if that were the invention of the Islamic Republic. Of course this isn't true—it's ridiculous to have to say so, but this perception of Iran is so widespread. Think of the conflict depicted in *Lawrence of Arabia*—that's a proxy war where Britain worked with Arabs to bring down the Ottoman Empire. The United States has a long history of proxy work, of course: the Contras in Nicaragua, the Mujahideen in Afghanistan. So yes, Iran has worked through proxies, but it did not invent this policy. It's a practice that both imperial actors and regional actors have long been using, and we have to think about the Middle East as a region. It's just too simplistic to say everyone is doing good except for one rogue state that is destabilizing everything. It just doesn't add up.

SHAMS: I want to turn to what's happening on the ground in Iran. Naghmeh, you've been translating articles by Iranian intellectuals and cultural figures on your blog, These Are the True Things, as well as for

Boston Review. Can you tell us about that project? What are you hearing these days? How are people in Iran experiencing this war right now?

SOHRABI: The idea came out of my own shortcomings. I noticed I was treating Iran basically like a primary source, reading texts produced there and incorporating them into my own writing for the information they contained. I thought, why are we not treating the analyses coming out of Iran on a par with our own analyses, particularly since those analyses are based on the lived experience of the people there? Why can't we let these voices speak for themselves? Lived experience qualitatively changes the kinds of analyses that we produce. The day I had that realization, I started translating.

"Anti-imperialism without feminism can easily collapse into support for authoritarianism, but feminism without anti-imperialism becomes cheerleading for empire."

Most of what I've translated has been analytical rather than personal reflections, such as investigative journalism, analyses of Iran's economic or political challenges published on various scholars' social media accounts, and so on. But today somebody reached out and shared a beautiful, heartbreaking letter they had written to a friend. I translated it because the writer just wanted to be heard—and I think when you're in a situation like Iranians are in now, simply getting the chance to be heard, even if the world is doing nothing to stop the bombs from falling, matters.

As for what I'm hearing, two things stand out. One is what Manijeh just mentioned: the notion of *estisal*. Loosely translated, the word means desperation, but there's a deeper sense that gets lost in that translation, and the idea now has a very specific historical association. It started to be used widely after the Twelve-Day War last year, and then again after the government's killing of protesters in January. The people I follow and translate are interested in *estisal* because they're thinking past the war. What they're saying is that we need to confront this sense of desperation that led so many Iranians to support the war in hopes that it would topple the government—both as a political issue and also even within our families, because a lot of families have been torn up over this.

Second is the notion that you can walk and chew gum at the same time: you can be simultaneously against the Islamic Republic and against this war. It is exasperating that so many feel we have to pick one of these things over the other, when the people who are actually experiencing the violence—which has been going on not since the outbreak of war on February 28 but before that in January, and before that in December, when the rial fell, and before that during the Twelve-Day War, and before that during the Woman, Life, Freedom movement—are able to say that being antiwar isn't conditional on the Islamic Republic's actions and that we can oppose both the war and the government at the same time. It behooves us to learn and do that simultaneously.

SHAMS: Peyman, you've written extensively about social and worker movements in Iran. Can you walk us through what was happening before this war, especially the protest movements on the ground, and broadly how things have unfolded since the end of the U.S.-Israeli attack last June?

JAFARI: Iran has a rich history of social movements and struggles; multiple waves of protests have arisen during the last four decades around political, social, cultural, economic, and ecological grievances, and sometimes these issues have overlapped and converged into movements.

Broadly speaking, we can distinguish three formations. First are workplace-oriented protests. Neoliberalization in Iran has meant that many workers face temporary contracts, low wages and pensions, and rising living costs. Groups that have protested include teachers, bus and truck drivers, workers in large industries such as steel and oil, as well as retirees, who have been a constant fixture on the streets in the last few years. (In fact, these include some of the main groups that have opposed both the Islamic Republic and the war—the national teachers' union, the bus drivers' union of Tehran, and the union of the Haft Tappeh sugarcane factory in southern Iran have all explicitly taken a position against the war.) Second are social movements outside and beyond the workplace, active around issues such as gender equality, environmental degradation, and academic freedom—the student movement, for instance. And third are street protests, sometimes converging with social movements and economic protests in revolts that target the political system as such.

In 2017 and early 2018, inflation sparked protests. In 2019, protests were triggered by a fuel price hike. Late 2022 saw the Woman, Life, Freedom movement, which was converging on many of these issues. And in January this year, mass protests were triggered by the devaluation of the rial and rising inflation once again.

There is so much to say about each of these formations and their interactions, but let me highlight one issue that has shaped all three: external threat in the form of sanctions and war. Economic sanctions imposed by the United States have exacerbated corruption, mismanagement, and social inequalities, triggering several revolts. At the same time, they have empowered and strengthened political and military elites while undermining movements' organizational capacity and transformative potential. And as a result, movements don't figure as centrally as they should in opposition to the Islamic Republic. This partially stems from *estisal*, that sense of frustration, which has led many Iranians not to see any way out but war.

The Woman, Life, Freedom movement is a case in point. It seriously limited the ability of authorities to enforce hijab rules in public space. But it has not gotten the kind of attention it deserves, both inside and outside Iran, not only because of *estisal* but because of a reactionary politics dead set on liberation from above instead of from below. The monarchists, especially, tried to sideline the movement because it offered an inclusive and emancipatory alternative to their own vision. Rather than dismissing such movements, we need to take them seriously and discuss how they can challenge the Islamic Republic more effectively. What kind of small victories can we win that will raise the confidence of the movement so it draws in more people and gains momentum? While the fall of the Islamic Republic is the end goal, it is important to think about concrete steps in between and provide the organization and leadership necessary to move these movements forward.

SHAMS: Speaking of Iranian support for the war, I'd like to broaden the picture and discuss the global Iranian diaspora. People around the world who have been following the war on social media have seen videos of diaspora

Iranians dancing in celebration. They've also seen videos of Iranian civilians being killed on the ground. Meanwhile, Reza Pahlavi, the exiled son of the Shah deposed in the 1979 revolution, has gained global visibility as he positions himself as a leader of the Iranian opposition. Manijeh, you've written a great deal on the history of the diaspora, and especially the Iranian left; help us understand these different reactions at this moment.

MORADIAN: The Iranian diaspora is deeply polarized. The loudest voices are the ones with money and access to mass media, so the segments of the diaspora that are committed to Zionist and monarchist ideologies have had the biggest platforms. Satellite TV stations like Iran International and Manoto, watched widely in the diaspora but also in Iran, have been perpetuating a kind of pro-war, pro-Israel, anti-Muslim, pro-Shah propaganda for a very long time, and over the last year, through the June war and the January massacres, it has gained a new kind of momentum inside Iran it didn't have before. It's been profoundly disturbing to see so many diaspora Iranians in the grip of a right-wing frenzy, cheering for war, utterly aligned with Trump and Netanyahu in callous disregard for the actual human beings in Iran.

"This conceit of Iran's unchangingness is premised on the idea that as long as you have clerics in charge, it's just more of the same: constant, top-down brutality. In fact, the Iranian political system has changed in important ways since 1979."

But aside from all this and the "Make Iran Great Again" insanity, there's an even larger swath of the diaspora that supports this war simply because they and their families have, in one way or another, suffered at the hands of the Islamic Republic. In other words, they support the war because they don't support the Islamic Republic. I think the key question comes back to this: How do we develop a political alternative that can respond to the real, legitimate grievances that people, in this case in the diaspora, have against the Islamic Republic, and channel that anger and hopelessness away from support for imperialist war?

There are people trying to do this. I'm a member of Feminists for Jina, a global network formed to support the Woman, Life, Freedom uprising that has consistently opposed the U.S.-Israeli wars on Iran, in June and now. We had a very long meeting yesterday trying to figure out how to keep raising our voices against war and state repression simultaneously, how to organize more people to take action, and I know we're not alone. I've seen many efforts in different registers to demand an immediate end to this war. I've seen petitions for ceasefire proposals in the UN. Some may be critical of that, but people are trying; it's one arena of struggle. Maybe it's pointless—we've seen the whole world let the genocide in Gaza happen. But silence doesn't seem like a good thing either. I've seen efforts to launch social media campaigns around war crimes. And almost every day, I get messages from Iranians in the diaspora saying, What do we do? How do we organize? Can we have a teach-in? Who's doing what? Connect me. I want to oppose this war.

There is thus a big political opening for a meaningful antiwar movement. The sheer scale of the destruction happening in Iran will push more and more of the diaspora to want to take a stand against it. But again, they won't want to do so in a way that seems like support for the regime. How, then, do we create the organizing spaces, the campaigns, the initiatives, online and on the ground, in the United States—the country that's doing the bombing—where we can unite against this war and bring people together while foregrounding an ethics of liberation and self-determination? I think getting serious about this is our only hope of shifting the discourse and the sentiments in the diaspora away from these truly frightening right-wing forces, these fascistic elements across the globe, and toward something that can respond to the multiple crises threatening the future of Iranians and us all.

SHAMS: I want to take us back into Iran and to the question of oil. All eyes have been on the Strait of Hormuz. Shutting it down and impacting global oil markets appears to be Iran's main strategy for spreading the pain globally. At the same time, the United States and Israel have attacked Iran's oil installations, including in Asaluyeh, which hosted a major workers' strike in January. Peyman, can you expand on the role of oil in this conflict, as well as the oil workers on the ground who are so often forgotten in these discussions?

Jafari: Let me start with the oil workers. They played a pivotal role in the 1979 revolution, but as Naghmeh pointed out, Iran has changed. The 1980s saw widespread repression, but the oil workers' strike in 1997 helped revive the labor movement in Iran. More recently, in 2022, oil and petrochemical workers in Asaluyeh and Mahshahr staged strikes in solidarity with the Woman, Life, Freedom movement. It is therefore perversely ironic that American and Israeli bombs—weapons that are supposed to be liberating the repressed people of Iran—have been falling on Asaluyeh and Mahshahr. At least five workers died yesterday in Mahshahr, and dozens more have been taken to the hospital. Thousands of workers have lost their jobs, both in Asaluyeh and in the steel factories of Ahvaz and Mahshahr. And these were impoverished communities to begin with.

So many communities depend on the petrochemical industry. These are civilian economic infrastructures, and harming them harms the larger population. For instance, Asaluyeh is home to the South Pars gas field, which delivers 70 percent of the consumption gas for the Iranian population. Over the last few decades, Iran has invested a tremendous amount in its petrochemical industry, which is now responsible for over 40 percent of its non-oil exports. Targeting this infrastructure has only one goal: the economic implosion of Iran.

On this score, it's worth recalling the "dual-use" argument invoked as a rationale for these attacks: the idea that, since infrastructure provides fuel to Iran's military, it is a legitimate target. The concept of dual use was introduced in order to protect civilians. But the United States and Israel have reversed the logic: if something is primarily for civilian use but has some kind of military use, too, they justify it as a legitimate target. The same reasoning has been applied to universities and other academic institutions.

Putting all this together, I think it's hard to deny this war is aimed at making postwar reconstruction impossible. The goal is to create a situation comparable not to Iraq in 2003 but to Iraq in 1991. Following the Gulf War, sanctions, cruise missile attacks, and bombardments led to a decade of social devastation and political chaos. And as it was then, the main victims of economic implosion and a failed state will be ordinary people and the undermining of their democratic struggles.

Shams: And now the United States and Israel have bombed one of Iran's main steel plants—more evidence that the goal isn't just to weaken the government but to deindustrialize Iran more broadly. Ali, in your recent article, "The Factory Was Always the Target," you describe how the United States has long sought to undermine Iran's quest for industrial independence. How do you understand what we're seeing today within the broader fate of U.S. global dominance?

Kadivar: You're right, Iranian infrastructure has been intentionally targeted. The steel plant; the Pasteur Institute, where Iran produces millions of doses of its own vaccines each year for domestic consumption and export; Sharif University of Technology was bombed today, too. What we are seeing is the deliberate destruction of Iran's industrial capacity and productive capacity, and all of it has a long historical shadow. This is where the historical arc I opened with matters.

"It's becoming clearer and clearer to masses of people that you can't just order a nice, clean war that takes out whoever you don't like and creates the political order you'd like."

The history of the steel plant is particularly revealing. Iran first attempted to build its own steel plant in the late 1930s under Reza Shah as part of his modernization programs. He couldn't get help from Britain or the United States, so he contracted with the Germans to build a steel plant in Karaj. Construction began, but then came the Anglo-Soviet occupation in 1941 and the deposing of Reza Shah. Even after the war, the Allies intercepted materials at sea and refused to let construction continue.

Both Trump and Netanyahu have spoken of regime change, but we shouldn't forget this has already happened in Iran—several times. In 1921 Reza Shah rose to power through a coup supported by Britain. The occupation in 1941 led to the removal of the head of state and the installation of a regime the UK and Soviets supported, although they still didn't support Mohammad Reza Shah's industrialization policies. In 1951 came the democratically elected premiership of Mohammed Mosaddegh, the secular prime minister. But when he nationalized oil, we saw a similar response from the West: instituting sanctions and embargos on Iranian oil, and refusing to provide technicians and parts for an oil industry that Iranians now wanted to run on their own. And then Mosaddegh was toppled in 1953 and the Shah was reinstalled, essentially as an American client. He posed no threat—Iran's nuclear program also hadn't started—and again tried to pursue industrialization, requesting a loan from the World Bank twice. He was turned down both times. Iran had to go to the Soviet Union to get support to build a steel plant in Isfahan—the same one that was just bombed.

The pattern couldn't be clearer. Four governments, with different regimes and different ideologies, but the same response from the West every time: refusing Iranian industrialization. There's no hard-coded reason it has to be this way—no reason that Iran and the West cannot work together. It's just the geopolitics of modern imperialism. For more than eight decades the United States has insisted on being the global hegemon, which entails keeping other countries from becoming independent and pursuing their own policies. It lost that bid with China, and it doesn't intend to allow another major power to rise if it can help it. But what is Iran? It's a large country with a big population. It's sitting on vast resources of oil and gas. It's educated in terms of geopolitics. It has connections to the subcontinent, to Central Asia, to the Caucasus, to the Middle East. For all these reasons, the U.S. foreign policy establishment simply can't tolerate Iran's independence, whether political or industrial and developmental.

SHAMS: I want to end on a different note. For so many people, this moment really feels hopeless. Where do you see alternatives to the darkness of the present emerging? Do you see reasons for hope in this moment?

SOHRABI: I'm just going to be honest: I'm heartbroken. It didn't have to be this way, for all the reasons that have been laid out. And I'm heartbroken not just for the thousands of people who have died and their families and friends but for the 92 million people in Iran who are scared all the time. The whole country hasn't slept for over a month. It's obvious but bears repeating: the vast majority of Americans simply can't imagine what it feels like to live under aerial bombardment. The fear is not only that you're going to die; at least when you die, it's over. The fear is that the bomb will fall two streets over. That sound is something you never forget. As one of the authors I translated said, it continues to live in your body. I think it's going to be really dark when this war is over—dark economically and dark politically. But the Iranian people haven't given up hope, and as long as they don't, I'm not going to either.

KADIVAR: One positive development may be the discrediting, in the eyes of large segments of ordinary people, of fantasies like regime change—the brute reliance on geopolitical pressure and imperial intervention. All this was sold as an easy project. The idea was that Trump would simply take out Khamenei, bomb the navy and air force and more nuclear sites, and the regime would collapse; a plane would bring Reza Pahlavi back, and Iran would be just like before 1979. A lot of AI-generated videos have circulated depicting just this. But it's becoming clearer and clearer to masses of people that you can't just order a nice, clean war that takes out whoever you don't like and creates the political order you'd like. We can have hope that this type of delusional politics is being recognized for what it is.

JAFARI: It's frustrating to be asked to come up with solutions, right? There are a bunch of pyromaniacs setting the world on fire, and then we are asked to put out the conflagration. Nevertheless, it's important to try to exercise agency. Mutual aid, people helping each other and trying to survive practically, is one area providing some hope for what is possible. On a more political level, we can take antiwar activism very seriously and organize it independently from the Islamic Republic. Getting out in the streets and opposing the war helps demonstrate who's really antiwar, both in the United States and in Iran.

MORADIAN: I keep going back to the famous Gramsci quote: the old world is dying, and the new struggles to be born, so it's producing these "morbid phenomena," fascism and war and genocide. I think hope has to be grounded in a sober assessment of how we got here—the fact that this wasn't inevitable. Embedded within that feeling of *estisal* is experience of struggle despite it all: war, sanctions, the internal repression. What gives me any kind of hope is that Iranians have been struggling for freedom and self-determination for a very long time. This is a moment of defeat, but it won't last forever. **BR**

Image: Getty Images

SOVEREIGNTY'S END AND BEGINNING

Farah Bakaari

THE LAST TIME I was able to go home was ten years ago, when I had just finished my first year of college. It would take me about fifty hours to travel from central Iowa to the Horn of Africa. Though I would eventually end up in Somaliland, where I was born and where my parents live, I had to first stop in neighboring Djibouti for an appointment at the U.S. embassy to interview for my re-entry visa. The visa would take three months to process, months I would spend in Somaliland trying to get reacquainted with my parents but mostly watching Bollywood movies and Turkish soaps dubbed in Arabic and eating with an acute awareness of my imminent return to the Midwest. At the end of summer my visa was ready, and I flew to Djibouti to pick it up before heading back to the States. At the embassy, the agent didn't stamp my passport. Instead, she stamped a piece of paper, which she then folded in half, in half again, then stapled inside my passport. Printed somewhere in the back of this paper were the words: "The below named traveler has a passport that is not recognized by the U.S. Department of State or has had the passport requirement waived. This visa is being issued per 22 CFR 41.113(b)."

The absurdity of this little diplomatic gymnastic has always struck me as both deeply humiliating and deeply hilarious. How could an otherwise empty piece of paper be deemed more worthwhile, more trustworthy than my passport, which bore the seal of the Republic of Somaliland? Did the agent know what it cost? That, although no country in the world at the time recognized Somaliland's sovereignty, hundreds of thousands of people had died for its name? But it had also been funny because the non-passport had done what all passports do: helped me cross one border into another as if by magic, in my case from what was, by all measures, an unknown, unwanted corner of the world into the heart of the American empire. The passport was both symbol and its negative, its power cemented in the very moment it was declared moot. Only a Somali could appreciate the perverse humor in this double irony.

But living through one perverse irony does not prepare you for another, or so I was reminded last December, when I woke up in my Berkeley apartment to the news that Israel had become the first country in the world to officially recognize Somaliland as a sovereign state. With the deal, capped off by a televised video call between Benjamin Netanyahu and Somaliland's president, Abdirahman Mohamed Abdullahi "Irro," Somaliland had at last received the kind of recognition it had been after for more than three decades. But rather than coming from any of its neighbors or from another postcolonial nation, that recognition was handed down by an occupying genocidal state that has worked tirelessly to destroy another people's right to self-determination.

"DOES ANYONE KNOW what Somaliland is?" Trump asked reporters when told of Israel's decision. Among those in the United States who heard the news at all, I suspect that many had a similar incredulity. Even more people, I'm sure, wondered just what Israel, of all countries, wanted to do with this obscure African territory. Answers to both these questions, I think, begin with the question of *where*.

Nestled just beneath the Horn of Africa's tip, the self-declared Republic of Somaliland shares borders with Ethiopia and Djibouti to its west and south. To its east is Somalia, which, along with the rest of the international community, considers Somaliland to be a semi-autonomous territory of its own nation. Since it unilaterally seceded from Somalia in 1991 following the bloody fall of Siad Barre's military regime, Somaliland has struggled to gain international recognition despite maintaining no formal ties with Somalia and donning all the trappings of statehood: an army, police force, governing bodies, elections, currency, passports. It even maintains diplomatic mission offices in several countries, including the United States, and periodically receives official representatives of others.

Somaliland received the recognition of statehood it had sought for decades—yet it came from a genocidal state that has worked tirelessly to destroy another people's right to self-determination.

None of these bureaucratic fixtures, however, measure up to Somaliland's 850 kilometers of coastline along the Gulf of Aden facing the Bab al-Mandab strait, where the Red Sea connects the Indian Ocean to the Mediterranean Sea through the Suez Canal—the waterway through which about a third of global container traffic passes. The current closure of the Strait of Hormuz by Iran as a tactic in its war with the United States and Israel is an acute reminder of the critical leverage these chokepoints offer in an increasingly interconnected, increasingly volatile geopolitical landscape. Somaliland has long understood its coastline to be its ticket to securing international recognition.

In 2016, the Dubai-based multi-national logistics company DP World signed a $442 million deal to build and operate a major logistics hub in Somaliland's Port of Berbera. In 2018, Russia was purportedly in talks with Somaliland to establish a naval base in the historic port town of Zaila, next door to Djibouti (where several western states, including the

United States, France, and Italy, maintain military bases) in exchange for diplomatic recognition. In 2024, Somaliland signed a memorandum of understanding with Ethiopia that granted the most populous landlocked country in the world access to the sea in exchange for future recognition of Somaliland's statehood. Yet after Somalia protested the move, calling the memorandum a violation of its territorial sovereignty, recalling its ambassador to Ethiopia, and threatening to send home all Ethiopian peacekeeping troops present in its territories, Ethiopia quietly backed out and publicly reaffirmed its support for Somalia.

Israel, seemingly unencumbered by such delicate diplomatic concerns, sees in Somaliland a golden opportunity. By establishing a presence in the Red Sea, Israel can monitor and counteract the Iran-backed Houthis, who have launched their attacks on Israeli shipping vessels from neighboring Yemen. Israeli presence on the Horn also has implications for the Saudi-UAE political rivalry in the peninsula. And it has the potential, too, to undermine the rising influence of Turkey and Egypt in the region. Last March, the Associated Press reported that the United States had reached out to three Muslim-majority African countries—Sudan, Somalia, and Somaliland—to inquire about the possibility of resettling two million Gazan refugees within their borders. Somaliland has thus far denied any such conversations took place, but that hasn't stopped many from interpreting Israel's recognition as a part of its grand displacement scheme.

Still, Israel's motives form only one side of the equation. It seems far more of a surprise, at least for anyone familiar with its political history, that Somaliland would so eagerly court Israel's friendship. But should it?

I WAS BORN AND RAISED in a small agricultural town called Gabiley about sixty kilometers west of Hargeisa, Somaliland's capital. Gabiley is the municipal town of a district that produces the majority of the country's food; the district is also the birthplace of many renowned poets and at least one Olympic gold medalist. When my parents were children in Gabiley, Somaliland was a British protectorate. By the time each, as teenagers, left town to try life elsewhere, Somaliland no longer existed, following the post-independence unification of Somaliland and Somalia in 1960, and

Gabiley was now part of the Federal Republic of Somalia. But the partial experiment of Soomaali Weyn, where all Somali-inhabited regions would unite under one republic, would quickly unravel, the intervening years marked by bitter divisions and tribal politics. And in 1969, less than a decade after independence, a coup d'état ushered in a brutal two-decade-long military dictatorship led by army general and former colonial officer Siad Barre. So, by the time I was born in 1995—the same year as Barre's death—Gabiley was once again part of Somaliland, now the name of the breakaway polity that cleaved itself off from Somalia alongside the old colonial borders. Somaliland and I were to grow up together, and we were each to behave as if the other had always existed.

In the late 1980s, at the height of the insurgent war against the military dictatorship, thousands of residents in Gabiley and its surrounding areas were apprehended without cause and summarily executed, their bodies dumped in unmarked mass graves as part of Barre's campaign of collective punishment of the Isaaq-majority northern regions, which were seeking independence. In what would later be referred to as the "Isaaq genocide," Barre ordered the complete destruction of the north, where the majority of the Isaaq clan's population lived. It is estimated that between 1987 and 1989, 200,000 people were killed, and millions more displaced. It is well documented how the strafing planes routinely followed civilians fleeing the violence and continued to bomb them at close range. As the resistance gained ground, the government intensified its tactics of collective punishment. The military targeted all the major water pumping systems in territories controlled by the opposition, sometimes going so far as to pollute the water sources with animal remains or sulfuric acid. They razed major cities, mined farms and grazing lands, poisoned the drinking water, seized civilian property, disappeared political dissidents, and massacred en masse. Barre had only one goal in mind: annihilation.

This was a genocidal campaign funded and given diplomatic cover by the United States government, which started supplying Barre with considerable military assistance as part of its Cold War agenda. After Somalia-Soviet relations broke down in 1977 following Somalia's invasion of Ethiopia over the contested Ogaden region, the United States saw an opportunity: over the next decade it would supply Barre with hundreds of millions in military assistance, in exchange for gaining access to Somali ports. In the wake of the Iranian Revolution, the United States wanted to preserve a military presence close to the Persian Gulf, no matter how cruel a despot they were supporting. If this is all starting to sound strangely familiar, I should add that one of Barre's lobbyist friends in the West was Paul Manafort, who, three decades later, would become chairman of Donald Trump's first presidential campaign.

Having been granted neither permission nor forgiveness for their act of self-determination, the people of Somaliland would need to decide what use they would put this history to.

Leading the insurgence against the military regime was the Somali National Movement (SNM), founded on a nonalignment platform that sought an end to all foreign military presence in the region. To defeat Barre, the SNM needed to broaden the base of anti-Barre insurgency within Somalia, forming alliances with other clan-based opposition groups in central and southern Somalia, including the United Somali Congress and the Somali Patriotic Movement. And although there were significant political and ideological differences among these groups and each had to contend with intra-group divisions, their coalition proved effective. In 1991, the military regime collapsed and Barre went into exile—at which point the SNM's coalition with other para-military groups dissolved. Rejecting the interim government, the SNM followed through with its separatist agenda and proceeded to unilaterally secede from Federal Republic of Somalia to form the Republic of Somaliland.

This is the wreckage out of which Somaliland's claim to sovereignty was fashioned. And having been granted neither permission nor forgiveness for their act of self-determination, the people of Somaliland would need to decide what kind of polity they would create with and for each other, to what use they would put this history.

CONSIDERING THE HOST of crises plaguing African states in the decades since formal independence—long-serving autocrats, civil wars, economic stagnation, environmental degradation—it's tempting to declare the postcolonial nation-state as having run out of political and theoretical steam. Such is the grim prognosis handed down, implicitly or explicitly, by much contemporary postcolonial scholarship, whose recent revisionist historiography has sought to show how the nation-state had foreclosed other forms post-imperial freedom could have taken. Recent books by Adom Getachew, Frederick Cooper, and Gary Wilder, for instance, all return to the late imperial moment to consider how anticolonial African leaders, negotiating their contradictory desires between interdependence and autonomy, found in the nation-state an unhappy compromise.

But while the anticolonial struggle of the late imperial world might have considered more expansive, utopic forms of cultural and political autonomy—federalism, self-determination without state sovereignty, and other non-hierarchal forms of worldmaking—independence, in the end, took the form that it did. And to properly apprehend the African subjects' relationship to their political present requires that we take seriously their continued investment in this form, especially in the moments it proves contradictory, even destructive. What happens when the nation-state is the form given to history, the entity that binds our experience of political time? And what happens when the form of the nation-state is denied to those desperately seeking it?

It's been thirty-five years since secession, and in that time citizens of Somaliland rebuilt slowly, tenaciously, and in great isolation. They re-opened hospitals, held democratic elections where they enthusiastically invited international observers, honored the peaceful transfer of power, updated their passport with a biometric chip, made K-12 education free, sent envoys abroad, re-opened music venues, built a national library, organized national sporting events, experimented with state-planned health care, innovated mobile money. But subtending the pride of self-sufficiency and the daily labor of securing relative stability in a volatile region is the persistent awareness that if we just did everything we were supposed to do, if we remained on our best behavior, then maybe, just maybe, we would be let in from the cold and into the only club that matters: the one that guarantees the right to have rights. For Somaliland, sovereignty (de jure sovereignty, as it has been a de facto state since the turn of the millennium) hasn't just been a practical matter but an existential one as well.

DURING THE WAR, the national army's Fifth Brigade was stationed near Gabiley, presumably for the area's proximity to Ethiopia, where the SNM headquarters were located. The commander of the Fifth Brigade was the infamously ruthless lieutenant colonel Yusuf Abdi Ali "Tukeh" (The Crow) whose moniker refers to his signature command: "kill all but the crows." It is not a stretch to say that Tukeh and the conduct of which he was exemplar were responsible for the ruins that formed the landscape of my childhood. There was the dilapidated stadium across the primary school, where during recess we played yard games, where come evening adventurous teenagers met to explore tobacco, hashish, and each other, and where in the winter months the mad and the homeless took shelter. There was the half-functional guest house of my childhood home, which was not fully restored until after I hit puberty. Once, my sister and I found a litter of kittens in what had been the guest kitchen but to us and to the kittens was simply an undefined structure without a roof where my mother kept discarded furniture and various tools. There was my middle school Arabic teacher, a quiet, gentle man who, a few times a year, would fail to show up to school and instead wander half-naked about town, wailing and belligerent. On those days we would spend our free period in the stadium ruins, where, out of reverence and fear, we would not speak of our teacher. On the way home from school, we would pass HALO Trust workers dressed in their personal protective gear drawing what seemed like arbitrary lines on the sand in backroads and alleyways.

And yet, when I was growing up, I was told it was the insurgency, not the military, that was based in Gabiley, and that all the destruction our town suffered was a direct result of fending off Barre's brutality. That is, the merciless violence and mass executions were, yes, forms of collective punishment, but a punishment endured from a position of resistance and agency. Until very recently I believed this to be the case. But so far, I can only find evidence of Tukeh's presence, not the SNM's. It is true that Afraad—an Isaaq-majority militant group, initially part of the Western Somali Liberation Front, the government-backed guerilla warfare against Ethiopia, before splitting from WLSF to join forces with the recently established SNM—was founded in Gabiley. But by 1982, the Afraad had already moved to Ethiopia. Why, then, in a town where people rarely told stories about the war, did they tell this one, which was at best only partly true?

I suspect it has something to do with endings. While we did not talk about the ruins, or the madmen who roved the town in tattered camouflage holding decommissioned AK-47s, or the HALO signs, or the disappeared, we talked about what came after the violence: Somaliland. The nation-state was not only a consolation prize for what we lost but a metonym for an ongoing collective suffering that couldn't be spoken. Somaliland, even as it referred to an older colonial order to justify the legitimacy of its territorial borders, became a way to mark a beginning. By anointing themselves the seat of the insurgency, the people of my town had wanted to retroactively make themselves the willing soldiers of the new republic—its heroes and heirs, and therefore, its ideal subjects.

All countries mythologize their origins, and the story Somaliland told about its origins meant something to me. I had understood that those who fought for the nation's independence, both in the battlefield and in the poetic form, had understood themselves as part of the long human struggle for freedom and dignity. Buried in Gabiley is the anticolonial, anti-tribal poet Abdillahi Suldaan Mohammed Timacadde, after whom the town's public (and at the time only) high school was named. On the eve of Somaliland's independence from the British, as the new flag was hoisted, Timacadde sung his ode to liberty: "Kana Siib Kana Saar," *lower this flag and hoist this one in its place*. Later disillusioned with the postcolonial Somali state and the ways clannism had undermined the nationalist project, Timacadde wrote many more political poems, including the now classic "Dugsi Ma Leh Qabyaaladi," *there is no shelter in clannism*. Timacadde also wrote about imperialism and neocolonialism, penning not one but two poems on Patrice Lumumba's assassination, describing him as "Geesiga madow uma ogola guusha reer Yurub," *the brave Black man whose victory Europe refuses to concede*. And even though no one outside of the Somali-speaking world knew much about the great poet, he saw himself as responsible for the world. In primary school we were tasked with memorizing and reciting Timacadde's revolutionary poetry, thus inheriting the responsibility he assumed in and about the world.

In Somali political life, the poet and the revolutionary are often one and the same. In the 1970s, the late Mohamed Ibrahim Warsame Hadraawi, who is arguably the best-known Somali poet outside of the region, spent five years in the notorious Qansax Dheere prison for his anti-authoritarian poetry and plays, including the poem "Ha La Qalay Raqdeedaa" (The Killing of the She-Camel). The poem depicts the vicious slaughter and consumption of the lactating she-camel—a Somali symbol for sustenance and communal prosperity—by gluttonous and unjust forces. In the 1980s, Hadraawi joined the SNM and took arms against Barre's military dictatorship. But for Hadraawi, a commitment to Somaliland's sovereignty did not have to be antithetical to Somali fraternity; in fact, it depended on it. In 2000s, he embarked on Socdaalka Nabada (Peace Journey), where he traversed the peninsula on foot promoting peace, fellowship, and reconciliation.

Because the poet is the custodian of the people's language, he assumes certain duties to speak about and on behalf of the people. He gives form to the nation but is not bound by national borders. Hadraawi's first political poem, "Galangal," was not about Somali fraternity or on behalf of Somaliland nationalism but for Vietnam in solidarity with its struggle against Western imperialism. And in 1982, after the Israeli invasion of Lebanon, Hadraawi wrote a poem in praise of Palestinian resistance. He would later explain, "the Palestinian cause is the same as the Lebanese cause, the Somali cause, the Vietnamese cause. They are all connected. And we ought to understand that the day they win is the day we win and their loss is our loss."

It was from Hadraawi's and Timacadde's poetry of international solidarity that I understood the stakes of Somaliland's right to self-determination. Every time I joined an organizing effort, participated in a protest, signed a petition, wrote an editorial, cooked for a sit-in, spoke at a rally, I imagined myself carrying on this legacy. My freedom has to mean something to someone's freedom struggle because mine meant something to those who fought for it.

As I write this, well aware that I could easily draw the vengeful ire of not just this administration but also the one at home, I think of a black-and-white photograph depicting thousands of Somali women holding a rally in Mogadishu to demand the release of Angela Davis ahead of her trial in 1972. Did Davis know about these women? Did it matter? Or is what mattered that those women felt responsible for the world, that they imagined their freedom as contingent on the freedom of all the women in the world?

THIS IS THE HISTORY and the responsibility that was so cheaply traded with that fawning phone call between Netanyahu and Irro. In the days following the announcement, I watched in horror and disbelief the videos and images of exuberant crowds of my fellow countrymen celebrating. I bristled at the sight of young people wrapped in Israeli flags, the tall glass buildings in downtown Hargeisa illuminated in blue and white. On social media, I saw former classmates register their delight and, as several of them put it, "gratitude" for Israel's supposed bravery.

By anointing themselves the seat of the insurgency, the people of my town had wanted to retroactively make themselves the willing soldiers of the new republic—its heroes and heirs, and therefore, its ideal subjects.

As disbelief gave way to disgust then to disillusionment, I thought of the first two lines of Hadraawi's famous poem "Daalacan," written shortly after his release from prison as a contribution to the influential Dheelley series, a debate in poems on the question of Somali nationalism. An ode to the stubborn, self-evident human quest for freedom and to the unique responsibility of the poet to keep count, "Daalacan," begins with a declaration: "Ma da'furin ogaalkay / Xaska dabada maan gelin." I went looking for this poem of my early schooling, for an encounter with the poet's regard for national character, for what he imagines a Somali to be, for the way all of these are enacted by the poem itself. Indeed, I thought, were we not "bulsho duul, daacad iyo xishood badan" (a people known to be honest and humble), were we not "ogow doqonse maahee" (so easily tricked by tyrants), and where there is tyranny, were we not to "dib bay ugu muddaystaan / Dulmigiisu waw kayd" (keep count and hold on to it)?

In the last few months, I have tried to resist the charge of naivety I could easily levy against my own cruel attachments to my home. You see, Somaliland, in its past and present, had also been the form I gave to the series of accidents that determined my own place in history, and everything I had traded for my own personal acts of self-determination. Somaliland made me make sense.

Somaliland cannot bring an end to the suffering of the Palestinian people any more than Israel can coerce the United States or any other country into stamping Somaliland's passport. If anything, Israel has damaged Somaliland's case. Following its announcement, the United Nations Security Council held an emergency session, where fourteen out of its fifteen current member states denounced the decision to recognize Somaliland, deeming it a violation of the UN Charter and the African Union Constitutive Act. The African Union, Arab League, and Organization of Islamic Cooperation, among the many others, likewise condemned the move.

But Somaliland's unfortunate betrayal of its own history and founding ideals in its embrace of Israel tells us a great deal about the consequences of imagining political and cultural freedom as struggles for national sovereignty. For Somaliland, international recognition of its statehood isn't just symbolic or even strategic but profoundly existential—to the point where the form of the nation-state takes precedence over the very history from which the struggle for self-determination found its legitimacy. Deeming recognition the only real way to be a full member of the world's community, Somaliland has ceased to think of itself as part of and responsible to it. Here, symbol devolves into sign, for which history is nothing but an instrument for the telos of preordained form.

If the arbitrary nature of African borders attests to the fact that there is nothing natural or pre-ordained about the form of the nation-state, the continuous, contested redrawing of Somali territories reminds us that there is nothing symbolic about it either. I often think about how different and easier my life would be if the world deemed my Somaliland passport legitimate. I could visit my aging parents; I could go on holiday in the countries where my siblings reside and get to know my nieces and nephews; I could attend the Pan-African Biennale in Nairobi in September; I could swim in the Aegean Sea, hike the Lion's Head, revel in the smells of Darajani Bazaar. In short, I could be in the world—I could feel free. But these are things to do, modest bourgeois freedoms I could have with almost any other passport. In that freedom's absence, there remains the things to be, the use to which can I put this accident of history. For now, I can only join the poet in keeping count: "Runta aan u daadego / Ducda hadalku waa hee." **BR**

WAR'S QUEER FACE

Photographs and text by J. Lester Feder

Iuliia (left), from Russia, and Anastasiia, from Ukraine, met via Instagram and fled to Germany in 2022.

I **VISITED UKRAINE** for the first time in October 2013. The country was finalizing an agreement for closer ties with the European Union, and Russia was doing everything in its power to derail the pact. But covering that process was not my purpose. I was on my first assignment as the international LGBTQ+ rights correspondent for *BuzzFeed News*, and I'd come to report on a proposed "gay propaganda" ban in Ukraine similar to one adopted in Russia earlier that year. The legislation technically prohibited giving information about queer relationships to minors, but it has been used much more broadly to censor expression by LGBTQ+ people.

It turned out, however, that my story was not so separate from the fight over Ukraine's relationship with the EU. The signs were everywhere, literally. "ASSOCIATION WITH THE EU MEANS SAME-SEX MARRIAGE," read billboards on the streets of Kyiv, funded by an oligarch close to Vladimir Putin. Opponents of stronger ties with Europe derided the EU as "Gayropa." Protesters against closer EU ties carried signs emblazoned with butt-fucking stick figures and slogans like "Homosexuality is a threat to national security" while chanting a Russian rhyme translating to "Go to Europe through the ass." As the deadline to sign the agreement approached in late November, a prominent Russian lawmaker warned, "The EU will demand that Ukraine expand its gay culture, and gay pride parades will be held in Kyiv instead of Victory Parades."

"ASSOCIATION WITH THE EU MEANS SAME-SEX MARRIAGE," read billboards on the streets of Kyiv.

These efforts sought to exploit homophobia that was already widespread in Ukraine. Pride parades had been attacked by right-wing groups and canceled by government officials, and dozens of hate crimes against LGBTQ+ people had been reported. In 2012, Ukraine was ranked one of the worst countries for LGBTQ+ rights by ILGA-Europe, the continent's umbrella queer rights organization. Putin was betting this homegrown homophobia would trump the allure of economic growth and democratic openness offered by the EU, where marriage equality and other LGBTQ+ rights were rapidly expanding. Caught in the middle, queer Ukrainians understood they were on the front lines of a struggle between superpowers. "Now the fight [is] between East and West, Russia and Europe," Olena Shevchenko, executive director of the queer feminist organization Insight, told me at the time. "Ukraine is the field of the battle."

She was speaking metaphorically, but her words were prophetic. A few weeks after my visit, Ukraine's then-president, Viktor Yanukovych, announced he would cancel the treaty with Europe and sign a pact with Moscow instead. The move sparked the Euromaidan mass protests, named for Independence Square (Maidan Nezalezhnosti) in Kyiv where they began. In their wake, Yanukovych was driven from power in February 2014—an event Ukrainians call "the Revolution of Dignity"—and Russia responded with force. Russian troops took control of Crimea days later. It was not long before Russia began supporting proxy militias in Ukraine's eastern Donbas region, supplying both mercenaries and soldiers.

As the ensuing war raged on—it never really ended—Putin and other propagandists continued to frame Russia as a leading opponent of LGBTQ+ rights on the world stage. In the run-up to the 2014 Winter Olympics, hosted in the Russian resort city of Sochi, Putin took advantage of global protests against the "gay propaganda" law to position Russia as a standard-bearer for "traditional values," "traditional families," and "religious life." By the time Putin launched a full-scale invasion of Ukraine on February 24, 2022, it was clear that the war was also a war against queer people.

That night in February, Putin even said so. In a long speech announcing his "special military operation," he claimed the West had tried to "utterly destroy" Russia's "traditional values" by pushing "false values . . . that are directly leading to degradation and degeneration, because they are contrary to human nature." Seven months later, Putin's rhetoric was even more hysterical. Declaring the annexation of four Ukrainian regions, he accused "the dictatorship of the Western elites" of destroying "traditional values" through "reverse religion" and "real Satanism." Addressing "all citizens of Russia," he asked:

> Do we really want to see perversions that lead to degradation and extinction be imposed on children in our schools from the earliest years, for it to be drilled into them that there are supposedly some genders besides women and men, and offered the chance to undergo sex-change operations?

Russia's invasion of Ukraine is the first time a global superpower invaded another country with the explicit goal of rolling back LGBTQ+ rights.

But the response of queer Ukrainians has also been unlike anything the world has ever seen. Years of advocacy had already made Ukraine a more welcoming place for LGBTQ+ people by 2022, and the full-scale invasion supercharged the visibility of queer Ukrainians in public life. Over the last few years queer Ukrainians, including an unprecedented number of queer soldiers, have made themselves more visible in the press and on social media. Never before have so many queer people been out and able to speak publicly about their experiences while under attack.

Wanting to document their stories, I interviewed and made portraits with more than forty queer Ukrainians—soldiers, survivors of war crimes, humanitarian volunteers, and refugees—during trips to Ukraine and neighboring countries between March 2022 and December 2024. A selection of these photographs appears here. The people I met are old and young, trans- and cis-gender, athletes and physically disabled, single and coupled. Their accounts reveal how queer people can be uniquely vulnerable in conflict and how they can feel especially called to fight. Collectively, they show how queer people have fought back, organized a movement, and built solidarity even as they continued to confront discrimination. They also demonstrate what oral histories and community building can achieve. (In two cases of war crimes allegations, by Diana and Oleksii Polukhin, I conducted extensive additional reporting; both signed affidavits prepared by an Odesa-based human rights organization for submission to the International Criminal Court.)

It's much easier to ignore someone's story if you never look them in the eyes, and queer people's experiences of war have largely been invisible. Most recent wars have been fought in places where it is generally unsafe for queer people to come out. Over the twelve years I've reported on queer people in conflict—fleeing ISIS in Iraq and Syria, civil wars in East Africa, gang wars in Central America—I've usually had to shield their identities by using pseudonyms and obscuring their faces in photographs. And because queer people are often hidden during wartime, we are often excluded when peace returns. For queer people, visibility is power.

I finished this project in the early months of Donald Trump's second presidency as he flattered Putin while deploying a homegrown brand of homophobia and transphobia in his own campaign to dismantle democracy. When the world grows more dangerous, we must fight harder, on all fronts, for fundamental values, including the right of all people to live safely, freely, and openly as queer. As Ihor, a young gay medical student who came out in the media after serving as a combat medic, said to me, "On the front lines, any day could be our last. So this is the time to start changing our lives for the better." **BR**

Yurii Ochichenko (left) met Andrii Kravchuk, cofounder of Nash Svit, one of Ukraine's first gay and lesbian human rights groups, in Luhansk in 1995. After Russian forces declared a "People's Republic" there in 2014, the couple settled in Kyiv. On the fourth day of Russia's 2022 invasion, members of a Ukrainian defense unit showed up at their home, identifying themselves as part of a right-wing paramilitary group that had harassed Nash Svit for years. Ochichenko and Kravchuk were taken to a police station, where cops beat them, saying they weren't "real Ukrainians." "There are only two options," Kravchuk told me. "The country will be free and democratic and any kind of people will be able to live here, or it will be a dictatorship."

Russian soldiers stopped Oleksii Polukhin at a checkpoint in May 2022, two months into the occupation of Kherson. They forced him to unlock his phone, saw he had been gathering information about Russian military positions, and found LGBTQ+ Telegram channels. They stripped him naked on the street, purportedly to search for pro-Ukrainian tattoos. "What's your opinion about faggots in our city?" Polukhin told me they called out to a passerby. "All of them should be killed!" the man replied. Polukhin was beaten and held in a detention center, where guards brought him a dress. "Wear it or we will beat you to death," he says they told him. Repeatedly interrogated over the next year, he was one of 200 victims in a case brought in Ukrainian court against seven Russian soldiers for violating the laws of war.

I met Diana, fond of taking in strays, in late 2023, nearly a year after Ukrainian forces liberated Kherson. She recounted being detained and tortured after Russian soldiers confronted her in June 2022, demanding she get a Russian passport. When she was defiant, they ransacked her home and learned she was gay. A soldier hit and blindfolded her; they took her to a detention center, where, she told me, they beat and electrocuted her before ultimately releasing her with orders to spy. She was detained again four months later, when she says she narrowly survived a mass execution. "The fear is permanent," she told me. But, she added, "I will not leave the city. This place is mine."

After the 2022 invasion, Oksana's queer friends fled Mykolaiv, but she stayed to care for her disabled sister and bed-ridden parents. I met her when she was working with Gay Alliance Ukraine to open a shelter and humanitarian relief hub, especially for those fleeing from nearby Kherson, which Russian forces captured in the early days of the invasion. No one would rent her a space. One landlord walked away just before they signed the lease, she said, after learning it was for an LGBTQ+ organization. "I'm not afraid of anything," she said. "It's never too late to change things."

Sasha (left) and Adam, both trans, met in Moscow after their parents moved from Russian-occupied Ukraine in early 2022. Adam feared Russia's anti-LGBTQ+ laws and was terrified his family members would find out. "I think they would have sent me to a monastery for 'reeducation,'" he told me. With the help of a former teacher, the two fled to Kyiv. Border guards became hostile after hearing them speak Russian. Searching their phones, the guards discovered the teenagers were a couple. "Gay people are sick—why are you coming to our country?" they said. "Go to Gayropa."

Mary McCarthy attends a hearing of the Senate Watergate Committee in 1973. Image: Mike Lien/ New York Times Co./Archive Photos/Getty Images

THE NOVELISTS AND THE WARMONGERS

Andrew Holter

"I **CONFESS THAT WHEN** I went to Vietnam early in February I was looking for material damaging to the American interest, and that I found it, though often by accident or in the process of being briefed by an official."

So begins the first of the novelist and critic Mary McCarthy's extraordinary dispatches from the Vietnam War filed for the *New York Review of Books* between the spring of 1967 and the summer of 1968. Quickly collected and published as two books, *Vietnam* and *Hanoi*,

McCarthy's reporting on Vietnam proved some of the most controversial American journalism to emerge from the war. It was not that she exposed one of the many war crimes perpetrated by U.S. forces in Vietnam, as Seymour Hersh documented the My Lai massacre or Jonathan Schell wrote of the destruction of Ben Suc. Rather, her reporting depicted the war as something perhaps even more painful for many Americans to confront: a psychodrama of vanity and hubris that indicted the values of the "Greatest Generation" to which she belonged.

Descriptions of combat were hardly necessary to illustrate this, and in fact McCarthy—curiously for a war reporter—passed up opportunities to accompany U.S. soldiers on patrol. Soon after she arrived in South Vietnam, the revered correspondent Bernard Fall encouraged her to tag along with the Air Force on a bombing mission. The experience would help train her to "feel nothing" as a war reporter, he said. "Be completely detached." The idea revulsed her. "For a person like me, a natural civilian," she wrote, "insentience should be the last thing to strive for; detachment would equal indifference." McCarthy's biographer, Frances Kiernan, notes that only a few days after their conversation, Fall died after tripping a landmine—one of over sixty journalists killed during the war.

More than fifty years after the fall of Saigon, *Vietnam* and *Hanoi* are worth reading as much for what they suggest about the possibilities and liabilities of war correspondence as what they say about Vietnam. History and public opinion have validated McCarthy's assessment of U.S. involvement as a sordid imperial endeavor many times over; that much is settled. What writers can say or do about a war to end it, though, remains a worthy question. Few literary figures living in the West today are willing to confront it as directly as McCarthy did, and they, like her, are typically rewarded with the condescension of a loud and powerful segment of their peers. Sally Rooney's defense of Palestine Action—and the subsequent backlash—is a case in point.

THE NEW JOURNALISM of the 1960s enlivened reporting with techniques of autobiography and literary fiction: Tom Wolfe did it with hot rod enthusiasts; George Plimpton with professional football; Truman

Capote and Joan Didion even covered murders. But war, as it was unfolding? McCarthy's decision to go to Vietnam was a much greater test of New Journalism's premise, one that many critics would judge as a failure. Writing in *Washington Monthly* in 1974, future White House speechwriter James Fallows agreed that novelists had earned their keep in American journalism. But "Mary McCarthy's political writing shows the other side of the story," he averred: "the damage that can be done by a novelist with insufficient care for the facts."

Indicting the values of the "Greatest Generation," McCarthy's reporting depicted the war in Vietnam as a psychodrama of vanity and hubris.

One reporter who had seen it all saw it differently. Murray Kempton, a long-running columnist of the New York press and veteran of World War II, thought McCarthy's eye as a novelist had done exactly what it was supposed to in Vietnam. Here, also, her gender had prevailed: after decades of being patronized as a "lady writer" and worse by contemporaries like Norman Mailer and Norman Podhoretz, McCarthy's fine-tuned perception of her male interlocutors, military and civilian, allowed her to draw out insights that no one else had.

To Kempton, it was an epiphany. "McCarthy gave me a general formula for understanding the war which I had never had before," he said. "She did that war as if it were a failed marriage." The marriage, in this case, was not between the government of the United States and its client South Vietnam so much as the men responsible for planning and directing the war and the rest of the country to whom they sold it as a high-minded enterprise.

Vietnam was an enterprise all right, McCarthy discovered as soon as she touched down. The American presence had brought so much consumerism and speculation to Saigon that it was coming to resemble not just the United States but urban California, she thought; the city was "like a stewing Los Angeles, shading into Hollywood, Venice Beach, and Watts." Profiteering wafted through the air no less than the smell of napalm in the morning. While traveling by military cargo plane to Hue, she listened as two pilots discussed the real estate development they would pursue once Ho Chi Minh threw in the towel: "From the air, while they kept an eye out for [Viet Cong], they had surveyed the possibilities and had decided on Nha Trang—'beautiful sand beaches'—better than Cam Ranh Bay—a 'desert.'"

Camouflaging this baser vulgarity were the pretensions of professional expertise. Military and civilian intellectuals, not businessmen, were responsible for elevating the work of the war into something systematic and scientific. McCarthy detected dubious thought everywhere. There were the unscrupulous local contractors of the CIA's anticommunist indoctrination efforts, some of them trained at Michigan State. There was the Marine colonel pondering his "scale model, like a crèche, in papier-mâché of an ideal Vietnamese hamlet," complete with a miniature bronze statue of a dollar sign, like the golden calf. And there was the alleged political science—about as empirical as alchemy—behind the disastrous "strategic hamlet" initiative to win over rural villages from the Viet Cong. In Vietnam, McCarthy reported, the can-do and know-how of the idealistic Kennedy era had dead-ended in futility and moral corruption.

Certainly, as some critics charged, McCarthy was a snob. She made no attempt to hide or soften her disdain for almost every American she met in South Vietnam—the language she alleged they debased, the junk they left behind as opposed to the things they carried. If she focused so much on the aesthetics of the war, as it were—on words and surfaces—it was because she had given serious thought to the conclusions of her closest friend, Hannah Arendt, about the banality of evil and its accessories of euphemism and cliché.

Technocrats, academics, and other experts—the "new mandarins" scrutinized by Noam Chomsky in the *New York Review*—played an essential role in this obfuscation, McCarthy stressed. Consider the following passage in light of the endless whine of self-pitying, self-exculpatory sophistry we hear today from the Israeli establishment and its defenders:

> To political scientists . . . the word "genocide" is quite unsuitable to describe what is happening. Genocide is *deliberate*. . . . If the Viet Cong plants a bomb in a theater, that is an atrocity, but if the Americans bomb a village that is "different." When you ask how it is different, the answer is that the VC action was deliberate, while the U.S. action was accidental. But in what way accidental

> if the fliers saw the village and could assume there were people in it and knew from experience that the bombs could go off? Well, the fliers were really aiming at the Viet Cong; if they hit some civilians, that was unintentional—it just happened. But it happens all the time, doesn't it? Yes, but each time it is an accident. In the American view, no area bombing implies premeditation of the results that follow, while every grenade hurled by a Viet Cong is launched in conformance with a *theory* and therefore possesses will and consciousness.

To observe that these lines simply "hold up" is to risk a shameful minimization in itself. I hasten to add that as I write this, the satanic idea of building luxury waterfront property on the Gaza Strip is not the pipe dream of IDF soldiers but the expressed interest of the White House and its chillingly named "Board of Peace."

Of course, McCarthy didn't need to go to Vietnam to draw these particular conclusions, but the fact that she did—that she *could*—underscores the enormous disadvantage of war writers and resisters in the present. In Rooney's case of support for Palestine Action, the risk and legal jeopardy the author bravely assumed lay in an expression of solidarity, not in what she could testify to having seen or heard in Gaza herself, firsthand. So it is with Omar El Akkad, Isabella Hammad, Pankaj Mishra, and Ta-Nehisi Coates, to name a few of the novelists who have written with probity and lucidity about Gaza for an international audience. (*The Message*, Coates's latest book of nonfiction, includes an essay describing his experience in the West Bank and East Jerusalem in the spring of 2023.)

The point is, none of these figures could have made a trip like McCarthy's had they wanted to. Israel has forbidden even the staidest, establishment-credentialed reporters from visiting Gaza for over two years now, never mind critics and novelists. Palestinian journalists have had to report the nightmare on their own, with targets on their backs all the while; scores have been killed. Only a small, select group of media outlets—CNN, NBC, ABC—has been admitted, on the condition their reporters embed with the IDF. Speaking recently about this price of admission on NPR, a network reporter broadcasting from Tel Aviv was ambivalent. "Some access is better than no access," she claimed. That is a debatable proposition, though not debated nearly enough.

Israel's media blackout is not just a tacit admission that its actions in Gaza are unspeakable; it's evidence that governments have learned from Washington's sentimental attitude toward press freedom in Vietnam. With a little more censorship or secrecy, some might insist, American leaders might have managed to bomb Hanoi in peace. The same line is now being taken more or less explicitly about Gaza, updated for the age of TikTok to boot. "When I'm trying to make arguments in favor of, you know, for Israel, I realize I'm talking through a wall of dead children," former Obama speechwriter Sarah Hurwitz complained at a conference in November, referring to social media footage of Israeli atrocities.

McCarthy's critics condemned her refusal to separate polemic from reportage, but as New Journalism her portrait of South Vietnam is lively in the manner of Gore Vidal's treatment of the Republican National Convention in the fall of '68: we get a series of tawdry set pieces in which the author's superior intelligence and wit—and, in McCarthy's case, moral indignation—triumph over all comers. The approach, as her subjects might have said, was to kill them all and let readers of the *New York Review* sort them out.

"Be completely detached," she was told. The idea revulsed her. "Insentience should be the last thing to strive for; detachment would equal indifference."

Her account of North Vietnam is a different story—the prose loses some of its quicksilver as polemic gives way to introspection, possibly to the point of solipsism. By her own admission, she confused herself there. Her reports ended up providing more material to her critics and biographers than to the antiwar movement, much less to the North Vietnamese whom she believed were basically in the right.

To be sure, it was brave of her to go in the first place. Almost no American journalists had reported from Hanoi before her, and the threat of aerial bombardment was ever present. Again she didn't see combat—North Vietnamese officials never offered to take her—and again, no matter. "The meaning of a war, if it has one," she wrote, "ought to be discernible in the rear, where the values being defended are situated."

At the level of theory, at least, North Vietnamese communist values, aligned with the Soviet Union and Maoist China, had long disturbed McCarthy. In the 1930s and '40s she had been a partisan of the anti-Stalinist left, the origin of her longstanding enmity with playwright Lillian Hellman. (Truth-telling was again the issue: "every word she writes is a lie," McCarthy said of Hellman on *The Dick Cavett Show* in 1980—"including 'and' and 'the.'") On the ground, though, McCarthy found herself rather charmed by the beleaguered, hospitable people she met in Hanoi. Under the circumstances it must have been hard not to be. The only way for her to access North Vietnam was as a member of one of the "Peace Committees," international delegations wined, dined, and closely supervised for the sake of good public relations. She did rather less than she might have to inconvenience her hosts with questions.

Notably, she missed the torture. McCarthy's account of her meeting with two American prisoners of war at Hoa Lo Prison (the "Hanoi Hilton," POWs called it) is astonishingly hasty and unilluminating. One of them just rubbed her the wrong way. He seemed dopey and "servile," she wrote in her notes, and had voted for Barry Goldwater. He spoke of his fondness for Vietnamese candy. Lieutenant Colonel James Robinson "Robbie" Risner *was* a conservative, but he was no idiot; he had been tortured. McCarthy was watching a performance. When Risner wrote his own version of their meeting following seven years of imprisonment, he was nowhere near as discourteous to McCarthy as she had been to him. What's more, she took to the *New York Review* to write a self-exculpatory rebuttal, much longer than her original account.

To put this episode in perspective, McCarthy's fellow *New York Review* contributor Susan Sontag was so disturbed and confused by her own meeting with American POWs in Hanoi in May 1968—recounted in "Trip to Hanoi," published first in *Esquire* and then as a book—that she chose not to write about the episode at all. "I was really dumb in those days," Sontag said many years later. "But I still had my instincts and I thought, This is a terrible situation. I don't understand it and I don't know what's right. So I didn't deal with it in my book."

McCarthy could hardly be faulted for not having recognized the signs of Risner's torture, as even young Fallows, her most perceptive critic, had to concede. Little was known about this subject in 1968, and there was some complexity to the way servicemen handled the ordeal of Hoa Lo, making the "terrible situation" opaque even from close up. McCarthy might have staked the politically coherent position that captured U.S. airmen were simply beyond the reach of her sympathy, responsible as they were for the millions of tons' worth of bombs dropped on civilian populations in Southeast Asia. However one sees it, the crucial missing element in McCarthy's account of Hoa Lo seems to have been curiosity about the facts. She let America get too much in her way.

Or did she? Just months before McCarthy first went to Vietnam, John Steinbeck had gone to write a series of pro-war columns for *Newsday*. They turned out to be the last of his writings to be published before his death in 1968. The Nobel Prize winner, tales of fruit-pickers long behind him, had made "a fool of himself" there, McCarthy thought. Still earlier, though, in February 1966, Steinbeck had written an even less well-remembered string of reports from Israel. He was enamored with the nation but admitted that his powers as an observer had failed him in a crucial respect: everywhere he looked, America overlaid itself like a double image. In the Negev he couldn't help but think of the Texas panhandle, or Nevada, or Death Valley. He knew "the shadings, the nuance" of the place were passing him by. He'd traveled all that way just to be left wondering: "Did I see only America?"

Here we have a perfect illustration of how novelists, acting as reporters, can apprehend the essence of things even in confusion and ignorance. Hadn't Steinbeck actually conveyed an important historical and political truth about Israel and its affinity with the United States? About mutual identification with the "frontier" and the prerogative of manifest destiny?

McCarthy, we could say, likewise succeeded through failure in Vietnam. There was much about the country, the people, and the war that she did not see and made limited effort to understand. Clearer to her were the terribly dangerous "fantasies and illusions of American men," as Kempton put it, and her own hope against hope that a novelist could help stop the war by piercing them. Show me the writer, then or now, credible enough to insist she was wrong for trying. **BR**

HOW NOT TO ABOLISH ICE

Harsha Walia

CALLS TO ABOLISH ICE are as old as the agency itself. When it was established in 2003 by President George W. Bush with bipartisan support, ICE was meant to serve as the domestic arm of the U.S.-led global war on terror, the at-home counterpart to the merciless military operations in Iraq and Afghanistan. Community organizers, in turn, saw their demands to dismantle ICE as part of resisting "the war at home," the post-9/11 attacks on immigrants and those deemed "national security threats" through mass surveillance, racial profiling, incarceration in detention centers and black sites, expanded enforcement powers, and border securitization. Organizations like Desis Rising Up and Moving fought for, and subsequently won, an end to the "Muslim Registrations" of over 84,000 Muslim men and boys through the infamous National Security Entry-Exit Registration System, and launched community defense programs to free people from ICE detention.

Most people, however, likely first encountered the idea of abolishing ICE more than a decade later, during Donald Trump's first term. In 2018, when the Department of Justice implemented a "zero-tolerance" policy toward irregular border crossers that resulted in the criminal prosecution of adults and the separation of thousands of children from their families, some activists created a social media hashtag—#AbolishICE—that swelled into a viral campaign, making the idea familiar among a broader swath of the American left. In the process, though, some of the original idea's nuance got stripped away. For one thing, the agency tasked with enforcing the family separation at the border was not ICE but Customs and Border Protection (CBP), one of almost two dozen agencies within the behemoth Department of Homeland Security (DHS) created in the wake of 9/11. And ICE and CBP are not the only agencies with the power to police immigration: through various policing and detention agreements, more than 1,000 local and state law enforcement agencies throughout the country also have jurisdiction over migrants.

Today, as Trump's high-visibility deportation regime has cast ICE's abuses back into public view, calls to abolish ICE are back. And while most in the party have stuck to calculated bromides about reining in the agency's power, some Democrats have joined the chorus of voices calling to dismantle it. But what the past decades of immigration struggles have taught us is that we must learn to resist a singular focus on ICE as a rogue agency, looking instead to how the sprawling border policing apparatus has been built up over years as a bipartisan effort. We certainly do need to abolish ICE, but that cannot be the only goal. The agency's abuses are not new, not created by Republicans alone, and not distinct from other enforcement agencies: they are tethered to otherwise normalized carceral and militarized infrastructures that will persist even without it. Abolish ICE is part of a broader political project that strikes at the heart of the border.

PUBLIC OUTRAGE AT ICE has peaked during each Trump term, yet without the Democratic presidents who helped cement an immigration apparatus bent on expanding mass detention and deportation, criminalizing migration through prosecutions, and militarizing the border, Trump would not be presiding over an agency with such vast power and deep pockets. Every day ICE, which commands a budget larger than all other federal law enforcement agencies combined and most of the world's militaries, spends millions of dollars to surveil, separate, and incarcerate over one thousand families. Those capacities were not only already part of immigration enforcement before the creation of ICE—they had also long been deployed within the web of policing.

In the 1990s, Bill Clinton's "tough on immigration" strategy converged with "tough on crime" policies, widening the net for detention and deportation for those with minor convictions stemming from stop-and-frisk policing and the war on drugs. New laws fast-tracked deportation, expanded the list of deportable offenses, mandated detention in many instances, and imposed criminal penalties for unauthorized border crossings by entangling the criminal legal and immigration systems (commonly referred to as "crimmigration"). Deportation and detention expansion aided the rise of the prison-industrial complex, too, with criminalization, illegalization, and policies of austerity acting as conjoined forces. Clinton's administration also created the notorious 287(g) agreements, which deputized local law enforcement as immigration authorities to check immigration status and authorize administrative warrants, collapsing the material distinction between these different agencies and opening the doors to the modern-day police state.

Ever since then, rhetoric embracing "legal" immigrants, with the simultaneous vilification of "criminal" and "illegal" immigrants, has remained a Democratic policy pillar. By the first year of Obama's presidency, about half of the people ICE detained came through the "Criminal Alien Program," which uses collaborations between local law enforcement and federal immigration enforcement as a pipeline for expulsion. Obama also turbocharged the Secure Communities initiative, which linked over 1,000 local law enforcement jurisdictions with ICE and FBI databases, nearly doubling deportation rates. By 2014, about half of all federal criminal arrests were immigration-related. By the end of Obama's second term, the three million deportations he had overseen earned him the moniker of "deporter-in-chief."

In his first term, Trump increased funding for ICE, further militarized the border, authorized the deportation of immigrants convicted or accused of minor crimes, and implemented the internationally condemned zero tolerance policy at the border. Despite promises to the contrary, Biden increased deportations and detention still further: in his administration's first year, the number of immigrants jailed by ICE increased by 70 percent over the last year of Trump's first term. Then, amid the U.S.-Israeli genocide of Palestine, the 2024 Biden-Harris campaign harkened back to Bush-era rhetoric by emphasizing immigration as a domestic security issue.

So today, when more and more Democrats voice support for eliminating ICE, we should be wary. Certain calls for abolition are in reality a means to stabilize, not dismantle, the violence of immigration enforcement. A case in point is Michigan representative Shri Thanedar's

Abolish ICE Act. Introduced to some fanfare in the media, the bill simply reassigns most ICE duties and funding to DHS—hardly true abolition. Other Democrats opt for rhetorical sleight of hand, opposing "Trump's ICE" or, as summed up by Congressman Troy Carter, seeking to "abolish ICE as we know it today." For them, ICE's most spectacular excesses are epitomized in the image of former DHS secretary Kristi Noem slandering two white citizens, Renée Good and Alex Pretti, as "domestic terrorists" after they were fatally shot by officers for acting as legal observers. Many of the Democrats' proposed reforms, such as body cameras and increased training (the latter paraded as a response to police abuses of power since the days of the Kerner Commission in the 1960s), are the same failed police reforms weaponized to quell generations of Black-led movements, including the 2020 uprisings.

Certain calls to abolish ICE are in reality a means to stabilize, not dismantle, the violence of immigration enforcement.

In the case of body cameras, for example, studies show that police departments frequently control footage release, and there is no statistical evidence proving body cameras reduce officer force or increase officer accountability. Four CBP officers on the scene of Pretti's shooting already had body cameras (though the footage has still not been released). And yet, to appease widespread outrage, DHS announced body cameras would be issued to all agents in Minneapolis, and then nationwide once funding was available. Put simply, body cameras don't work *and* become a pretense for bloating enforcement budgets.

As political scientist Naomi Murakawa documents, the unprecedented number of legal reforms passed in the months following the murder of George Floyd gave the veneer of addressing police accountability but, in actuality, only shored up police legitimacy. Data from Mapping Police Violence shows that police-perpetrated killings have increased, not decreased, since 2020. Liberal conceit thus maintains the war of the carceral system, while ensuring capital flows for corporate giants like Geo Group, L3, Palantir, Axon, and Lockheed Martin. As journalists Maya Schenwar and Victoria Law describe, reform "is the re-forming of the system in its own image, using the same raw materials: white supremacy, a history of oppression, and a toolkit whose main contents are confinement, isolation, surveillance, and punishment."

Liberal reformism also perpetuates the erroneous assumption that police can be allies in the fight against ICE. Over the last year, there have been countless pleas for police officers to protect people from ICE, and many cities are reporting increases in 911 calls to report ICE activity. But ICE surges are often accompanied by local police or involve police information sharing and surveillance cooperation as force multipliers. Similarly, ICE detention capacity is largely expanding through existing Bureau of Prison facilities, the carceral carousel that just cycles prisons for different uses at different times. The binary between "good cop" and "bad ICE" launders the everyday carnage of police and prisons. Even further, there is no material or ideological distinction between ICE and police; both are an extension of the anti-Black warfare waged since the country's founding. The attempts to rein in irregular migration stem from the *longue durée* of the policing of Black mobility, described by Benjamin Ndugga-Kabuye and Tia Oso as the United States's central "pre-occupation with Black movement." Contemporary immigration enforcement draws heavily on the Fugitive Slave Acts of 1793 and 1850; in fact, one of the first operations of ICE in 2003 was called the "Fugitive Operations Program" to capture noncitizens who had gone underground.

Immigration enforcement is thus not in contrast to, or even parallel to, police; it *is* a method of policing. As far back as the 1980s, Ronald Reagan's administration identified the Immigration and Naturalization Service, the predecessor of DHS, as "a criminal justice agency." Today, there are over 1,400 federal 287(g) agreements with tens of thousands of local officers in a capillary network of immigration policing crossing forty states, and—even without high-profile ICE occupations in their cities—hundreds of local jails are ballooning with migrants snatched from their families through existing state-level agreements for immigration incarceration. At the same time, Trump has transferred stretches of borderlands to military jurisdiction with a deployment of over 20,000 troops. Immigration enforcement is an ever-expanding architecture that continuously collapses the local and global, seamlessly merging with both policing and military power.

It is not enough, then, to focus on the governance and oversight of ICE because the agency is not an anomaly. Instead, we must question *all* carceral systems that capture an expanding web of subjugated people. As abolitionist Mariame Kaba insists, the abolition of policing goes beyond the police, recognizing that child welfare reporting, drug courts, mandatory psychiatric treatment, and immigration detention are also forms of criminalization and control that are counter to providing meaningful safety. Abolishing ICE, then, is the floor towards abolishing all policing and carceral systems. Abolishing ICE also means permanent, full rights for migrants and abolishing the border itself—a structuring force for all immigration, policing, and military violence.

THE TERROR OF ICE home invasions, racially motivated man hunts by law enforcement, car chases at traffic stops, abandoned children in abandoned cars: these displays of naked brutality expose how the border can follow migrants anywhere. The infrastructure and ecosystem of entire towns are being reshaped by this moving border, which has ordered people, disappeared immigrants, paramilitarized neighborhoods, and turned cities into the borderlands. Today's border is elastic—at once domestic and global, internal and external.

For one, border policing extends well within the nation-state. Immigration agents, for instance, can be authorized to demand tenant information from landlords, healthcare and social workers are being conscripted into information sharing programs, and local policing agencies routinely enforce immigration warrants and detention. Even when migrants are released from detention, they are often forced to wear electronic ankle bracelets, the border mapped onto their bodies. The internalization of the border is perhaps most apparent with the 100-mile rule, in which CBP claims extended authority for warrantless searches and internal checkpoints within a 100-mile zone of any border, which includes the entire U.S. coast—multiplying the border into a radius where nearly two-thirds of the population resides.

Border internalization also affects the workplace. Despite the fact that immigrant workers labor alongside citizen workers, their immigration status makes them more vulnerable to employer exploitation. While the most visible consequence of ICE raids is the terror of expulsion, border enforcement is not actually intended to deport everyone. Every politician understands that deporting all undocumented immigrants would cause much of the economy to collapse. In a 2025 interview about farmworker deportations, Trump stated: "We can't let our farmers not have anybody." Borders create conditions of deportability, which produces labor precarity and keeps immigrant workers compliant. Following ICE raids last year, many undocumented workers in construction reported unscrupulous employers taking advantage of the climate of fear to reduce their wages and increase their workloads. The border is thus animated in the workplace, segmenting the labor force and acting as a spatial fix for capital accumulation. By shaping the state and capital's ability to deflate labor power and manage citizenship, the border always serves capital. Investors, diplomats, tourists, and soldiers move freely across borders while migrant labor is made precarious, preserving the long-standing distinction between propertied settler citizenship and exploited racialized subjugation.

The border is also externalized. Last year, in a $4.67 million detention outsourcing deal, the Trump administration paid Nayib Bukele's government in El Salvador to accept Venezuelan deportees, many of whom were then incarcerated in the infamous CECOT gulag. For years, the United States has funded immigration enforcement in El Salvador, Guatemala, Honduras, Mexico, Panama, Dominican Republic, Haiti, Colombia, Venezuela, Costa Rica, and elsewhere, with the aim of preventing migrants from ever reaching a U.S. border. Now, Trump is extending border outsourcing to third country deportations, making agreements with at least twenty-seven countries. Most recently, in April, a group of Colombians, Peruvians, and Ecuadorians were deported from the United States to the Democratic Republic of Congo. Not coincidentally, just a few months prior, the United States signed a partnership granting it preferential access to Congo's minerals. Many present-day bilateral agreements revolve around the same model: trade, investment, resource extraction, security partnerships, and migration prevention.

Much like the impacts of increased interior enforcement, the archipelago of outsourced borders has transformed the political economy—as well as the physical landscapes—of many Latin American and Caribbean countries. In Mexico, for example, migration policies are securitized with a sprawling carceral infrastructure, and over 100,000 officers deployed to apprehend, detain, and repatriate migrants. Known as the containment strategy and dictated by the United States through a series of bilateral and multilateral agreements, a battery of migration checkpoints manned by the army, police, and National Guard runs from the southern to northern border. The country also has one of the world's largest immigration detention systems. Migrants from across the hemisphere face arbitrary detentions, gendered violence, and illegal pushbacks. Parallel to the war on drugs, the agreements couple militarization with forced neoliberal restructuring by also imposing trade and investment policies serving elite interests.

Border outsourcing thus serves a myriad of functions: blockading irregular migration into the United States; circumventing legal obligations by claiming violations are outside U.S. jurisdiction; further cracking open countries for capitalist trade and extraction; and expanding the Monroe Doctrine by compelling governments to accept migrant interception checkpoints and offshore detention. Imperialism—through a long arc of dirty wars, coups, unfair trade agreements, and resource extraction—is already a root cause of migration. Now, border outsourcing is becoming a means of imperial management; it both globalizes border violence and maintains a colonial present.

This process is not entirely new. The most recent outsourcing of borders was pioneered by Europe thirty years ago: the EU spends billions on its sweeping externalization infrastructure across Europe, Africa, and Asia that not only creates a killing field for migrants but also props up authoritarianism, the global arms trade, and vast geographies of paramilitarization. In Sudan, for example, the EU-funded Khartoum Process began militarizing the Sahel and Horn border regions and financially backed the genocidal Rapid Support Forces to become EU border guards to stop migrants from crossing between Darfur and Libya and across the Mediterranean. In Libya today, the EU-backed Libyan Coastguard are notorious for widespread torture, forced labor, slavery, and sexual violence. Yet, the EU has allocated another €52 million for the next two years to support Libyan border securitization. Across Africa, there are 400 different EU migration prevention projects resourcing surveillance, military equipment, detention centers, border enforcement trainings, and interdiction. A similar pattern is repeating across West Asia and Eastern Europe. Turkey receives billions in EU aid and the possibility of accession into the EU in exchange for buffering against migrants passing through it into Greece. In Ukraine, the EU Eastern Partnership Program has paid for three new EU-funded detention centers and, similar to Libya, turned the country into EU's border guards to fortify Europe as a "white enclosure." Since the proclamation of a global refugee crisis in 2015, at least 27,000 migrants have drowned in the Mediterranean. (Aimé Césaire haunts: "Europe is indefensible.")

It is not just that white nationalism is ideological fodder for fascist forces. Rather, fascism *itself* is constituted through the quotidian violence of the border.

If the border is everywhere, then what exactly is the border? It is best understood not as a fixed line, but as an ordering regime of human immobility and labor discipline thickening across space and time to reproduce a global colonial order and stabilize racial capitalism. Abolishing ICE, then, necessitates abolishing the border wherever it proliferates, and dismantling the conditions spawning both the global crisis of displacement and a global empire of borders.

FASCISM IS AN OUTGROWTH of capitalist liberal democracies. The far right virulently demonizes criminalized and illegalized others, feeding off what most liberals believe to be the otherwise reasonable institution of borders—what Democrats call the "lawful administration of immigration" in contrast to the paramilitary violence of ICE. Yet there is nothing coherent about the definition of "criminal alien," "illegal," or "unauthorized arrival," discursive categories that are always shifted and policed to maintain cheapened labor and racial citizenship. In this way, the recent accounts of Indigenous people being apprehended by ICE are not ironic: in fact, some of the earliest political battles against immigration were launched by Crees, Chippewas, and Yaquis who, in the nineteenth century, were considered "illegal" by an expansionist settler state. Today, "illegal migrants" are scapegoated to deflect responsibility for austerity agendas and billionaire profits generating mass inequality.

It is not just that anti-immigration sentiment and white nationalism are the current ideological fodder for fascist forces. Rather, fascism *itself*—which relies on the idea of a homogeneous, exclusionary body politic—is constituted through the quotidian violence of the border, the perfect breeding ground for fantasies of ethnonationalism, cultural supremacy, racial purity, and Darwinian lifeboat survivalism. Simply put, because borders provide the ideological basis for fascism, being an antifascist means being a border abolitionist.

Today, displacement and the constriction of mobility has reached unprecedented levels; in the course of my lifetime, the global number of migrants has doubled. We are living through genocides from Palestine to Sudan, imperialist aggression and forever wars from Latin America to West Asia, unmitigated resource extraction on Indigenous lands amid climate catastrophe, and authoritarian attacks on diverse communities and on the very right to dissent. The linchpin in these concurrent wars normalizing mass death and disposability is border imperialism: a system of global apartheid upholding racialized class control within empire.

Witnessing these daily horrors, residents from Los Angeles to Chicago to Minneapolis are fighting the logic and materiality of borders, refusing to succumb to the multibillion-dollar industry of fascist propaganda and rejecting state violence that categorizes and brutalizes migrants. Whether through direct action, rapid response teams, care networks, mass coalition-building, national days of action, or mutual aid, these constellations of resistance push back against bordering and its dehumanizing differentiations between the state-constructed categories of migrant and citizen. Organizing allows us to see each other as coworkers and neighbors who share kinship and belonging, having more in common with each other and our siblings around the world than those who drew borders to rule us.

Already, the fascist agenda has suffered magnificent defeats. Organizers have compelled contractors Avelo Airlines, Pattison Group, Prairie Band Potawatomi Nation, and Oneida-Stantec to end partnerships with ICE and DHS; forced DHS to postpone plans for mass immigrant warehousing; gotten detention center construction and expansion banned in cities like Seattle; and undertaken many acts of defiance to prevent, delay, and otherwise hinder ICE enforcement and kidnappings in neighborhoods across the country. As abstract as it may sound, anti-border organizing is not simply a utopian horizon. Guided by an internationalist framework, it is an everyday presence working to render borders, and the violence they uphold, obsolete.

This moment is our compass. In the face of anti-migrant terror, our responses cannot be confined to diversity ethics, or platitudes about "good" or "innocent" immigrants; instead, we must reverse the gaze to confront the animating logic of bordering regimes. To abolish ICE, we must oppose bipartisan immigration enforcement as a key method of state violence, refuse the lure of reforms that preserve immigration and policing power, and dismantle bordering regimes that are a principal structuring force of racial capitalism and global empire. The abolition of borders is a necessary pillar to defeating fascism today, and an expansive vision for our collective liberation. **BR**

GOOD LIVES
Jan Grue

The Question of Unworthy Life: Eugenics and Germany's Twentieth Century
Dagmar Herzog
Princeton University Press, 2024

The Life Worth Living: Disability, Pain, and Morality
Joel Michael Reynolds
University of Minnesota Press, 2022

The Art of Flourishing: Conversations on Disability
Edited by Liz Bowen, Joel Michael Reynolds, Rosemarie Garland-Thomson, and Erik Parens
Oxford University Press, 2025

AT THE NUREMBERG MEDICAL TRIALS, Karl Brandt, Hitler's personal physician, testified about his involvement in what he referred to as "the Leipzig case." The parents of a child born with several disabilities wanted to have it killed. Since the director of their local hospital had rebuffed them, they had petitioned the Führer's chancellery directly. As it happened, the Führer wanted a solution to the so-called euthanasia question, and so Brandt was directed to review the case and make it an exemplar. He found, as he put it, no reason to let the child live.

The child, eventually identified as a boy named Gerhard Kretschmar, became the first known victim of the T4 program, which killed nearly 300,000 disabled people between 1939 and 1945. While public protests led to an official suspension of the program in 1941, T4 continued its practices unofficially, the "wild" phase of its "euthanasia" lasting until the end of the war. Even in the postwar years, there was a "crushing breadth of popular support for the perpetrators, and ongoing shaming of the victims and their families," writes historian Dagmar Herzog in *The Question of Unworthy Life*. Beyond Brandt, who was convicted of crimes against humanity at Nuremberg and executed in 1948, very few physicians were held accountable, while people with disabilities kept being marginalized, confined to underfunded and short-staffed institutions. Not infrequently, ex-Nazi employees were "hired back as nurses and wardens." Disabled people "were not viewed by their fellow citizens as fully human," writes Herzog, "and their lives, bodies, and souls were not treated as of equal value."

Much about the medical murders was known from the beginning; more was uncovered after the end of the war. Yet the revelations about the T4 program failed to banish one of its core assumptions: that some disabilities inherently make life not worth living. Is it an overstatement to say that echoes of that sentiment persist today? I don't think so. One doesn't need to look too closely to see traces of T4 in tech's transhumanist ambitions to overcome human frailty and bodily vulnerability once and for all.

Take Nucleus Genomics. Financed in part by Peter Thiel's Founders Fund, the company—which ran a major ad campaign last year using taglines like "IQ is 50% genetic"—offers screening of up to twenty IVF embryos with the promise of evading undesirable "genetic conditions and traits," among them somatic disorders like Huntington's, caused by single-gene mutations, as well as much more loosely defined conditions like ADHD, insomnia, alcoholism, and anxiety. The pitch is that prospective parents can have their "best baby," which in turn presupposes that such a thing exists.

This new eugenics is depressingly similar to its antecedents in its rejection of the body, and the granularity of embodied life, in favor of a narrow, singular vision of the life of the mind. Intelligence, narrowly defined, reigns supreme; bodily variation, like a clunky bit of code, is a problem in need of debugging. Unlike its forebears, though, the new order appears willing to let some of the would-be outcasts into the club—so long as they prove useful. Certain forms of neurodiversity have even been embraced, recast not as hindrances but superpowers, the mark of the mythical "10x" engineer who churns out work an order of magnitude more productively than "normal" workers. For tech moguls like Elon Musk and Alex Karp of Palantir, a hint of autism is perfectly acceptable, even desirable, if it strengthens the bottom line. According to Karp, only two kinds of people will succeed in the AI era: trade workers and the neurodivergent. Within the vastly diverse minority of disabled people, it has long been possible to discern the subgroup of the "able-disabled," the people who gain some degree of social acceptance by living up to productivity norms and demonstrating their economic utility, often at a high human cost.

According to this familiar logic, the disabled remainder might well be better off dead. In Jojo Moyes's bestselling novel *Me Before You* (2012), a rich, highly privileged quadriplegic man insists that he is nevertheless deprived of everything that makes life good, including the possibility of working, and must therefore kill himself. He does, and the story frames this as a happy ending. In 2021, Canada enacted laws that made nonterminal disabilities a sufficient, legitimate reason for physician-assisted suicide. And in one of the baldest statements of the cost-benefit approach, President Trump, after a meeting with disability advocates during his first term, allegedly said that, with the expenses involved, "those kinds of people"—referring to disabled people who required strict care and frequent hospital trips—"should just die."

One doesn't need to look too closely to see traces of the Nazi euthanasia program for the disabled in tech's transhumanist ambitions.

Haven't we made *some* progress, though? I've been hearing language like Trump's less often since I became a tenured professor, or for that matter since I got married and became a father. It seems I'm no longer being challenged, however implicitly, to prove that my life is worth living. Perhaps I'm passing as one of the able-disabled. Perhaps I'm now spending more time in the company of people who have lived long enough to think twice about what sort of experiences might really make you wish you were dead. And perhaps, following decades of activism, there has been a cultural shift in what "disability" signifies. From the 1960s onwards, American activists drew inspiration from and aligned with the civil rights movement to position disability as a minority identity. In the United Kingdom in the 1970s, the "social model" explained the marginalization of disabled people as a form of political and economic oppression driven by industrial capitalism and the privileging of interchangeable workers' bodies. In both cases, disability was reconfigured from an individual medical problem to a phenomenon with social, cultural, and historical aspects: as a binary category of exclusion imposed on the range of natural human variation. The year

I was born, 1981, happened to be the United Nations' International Year of Disabled Persons. In the decades since, anti-discrimination laws have been implemented across the world.

It can be hard to reconcile this cheerful story of social progress with the sudden, baleful resurgence of eugenic ideology. But eugenics arose, in part, as a progressive project aimed at bettering the human condition, and even modern, progressive disability policies have partly been motivated by the idea that disability can somehow be "solved." Some forms of the social model took the position that once political and economic oppression were eliminated, full equality would be achieved; the UN Convention on the Rights of Persons with Disabilities similarly advances the goal of "full and equal participation." Like any grand ideal, these bear an equally grand potential for disappointment. All utopias, Fredric Jameson once observed, are defined by what they exclude, and disability's utopian scenarios are no exception: they leave no room for the people who cannot live up to a particular standard, whether defined by productivity norms or some more humane understanding of lives well lived. The persistence of this gap in our thinking suggests there are still fundamental philosophical questions to be answered about how we view such people. Why we can only conceive of certain lives as problems to be remedied? Why, in short, does disability remain synonymous with deficit?

The Question of Unworthy Life is concerned with how twentieth-century medicalized killing became grounded in a generalized equation of disability with lack of value—and in particular, why "disabled people were not 'forgotten' victims, but rather aggressively repudiated ones." The T4 program was carried out in hospitals and asylums throughout Germany, and usually, unlike the case of Gerhard Kretschmar, against families' wishes. The death certificates that families received, indicating natural causes of death like heart failure, were often suspected to be false. The murders were sufficiently well known that open protests began to erupt in February 1941, and the program officially shut down in August of that year. But the killings didn't stop, and there was no real reckoning, neither legally nor morally. Only in the 1980s and

1990s was the "euthanasia" acknowledged as a mass crime. It was as late as 2014 that a national memorial was dedicated at Tiergartenstrasse 4 in Berlin, the address that gave the program its name.

What gave the ideology behind T4 such formidable reach and staying power? Herzog uncovers a deep set of intellectual roots. The term "unworthy lives" was coined in the first place in an infamous and highly influential 1920 pamphlet, *Die Freigabe der Vernichtung lebensunwerten Lebens* ("Allowing the destruction of life unworthy of living"), by the jurist Karl Binding and the psychiatrist Alfred Hoche. They argued that certain people could be legitimately killed not only because it benefited the economy, but for their own good. The pamphlet is sometimes referred to in contemporary debates about euthanasia and assisted suicide, usually as an outlier in terms of its ethical stance. Herzog renders it less exceptional, placing it in the context of ethical and political debates that were, in the late nineteenth and early twentieth century, framed around eugenic hierarchizations of human worth.

Binding and Hoche's reasoning was profoundly hypocritical. The pamphlet argues that people who suffer and want to end their lives should be helped to die, but so should people who don't understand how bleak and pointless their lives are. As it happened, the latter were the people who were also an economic burden on society. Herzog's most chilling passages describe victims who were deemed to lack human agency, but knew exactly what was happening to them. This includes Hans, a man living at an institution in Württemberg, who shouted to the personnel about to take him to the killing center: "Our blood be upon you!"

The Nazis' obsession with "useless eaters," like the T4 program itself, was grounded in a longstanding obsession with the costs and benefits of supporting the lives of disabled people. State investment in care or education could only be justified with an expected outcome of "some improved usefulness." In many countries in the nineteenth century, from the United States to Scandinavia, the emergence of some form of inclusive education grew from the idea that physically and intellectually disabled people could become productive citizens. When faced with limits to how "useful" some people would become, eugenically minded politicians as well as intellectuals began to explore other options.

As a host of disability scholars have pointed out, the idea of the useless or unproductive citizen is closely tied to industrialization and the individualized labor market. The political and economic forces that made possible the figure of the "useless eater" were the same that made every worker's labor replaceable. "Disability" is notoriously hard to define, but one of its aspects is having a smaller quantity of labor power to sell (or none at all), or being unable to sell it because places of work are organized around the human body perceived as "normal." In modern societies, this has often meant that disabled people must live on the sufferance of the state, receiving disability benefits, a stigma that reflects the moral and social primacy of economic productivity.

In the twenty-first century, these remain critical issues, certainly to the extent that access to quality health care depends on money. Under the T4 program, Herzog shows, some disabled people survived only because they could provide a modicum of labor in the institutions where they were kept. Their lives had no other value; they were circumscribed by the cost-benefit analysis that derived from the principles of "racial hygiene."

The German equivalent to Anglo-American "eugenics," the term was coined by the biologist Alfred Ploetz, who thought that superior peoples must be guarded both from the foreign bodies of inferior races and from the inferior representatives of their own kind. Here, as Herzog points out, lies the connection between the Nazis' view of Jews and their perception of disabled people. One threat was external, the other was internal, but both were antithetical to the purity of the master race. In approaching the inner threat, Ploetz drew on stories about the ancient Spartans, and the legendary mountain range Taygetus, where "unfit" infants would be disposed of. Like the Spartans, the Germanic people would become beautiful and strong, Ploetz thought, only by killing off the weak. Like Binding and Hoche's "humane" arguments for euthanasia, the notion of the good life was not just an ideal to strive for; it was also a criterion for identifying lives that were not worthy.

It would be a mistake, Herzog seems to warn us, to see eugenics as the only intellectual antecedent for the drive to eliminate disability: she points to Nietzsche's contention that it would be "more cruel" to let a disabled infant live than to kill it and Martin Luther's stance that a disabled child could be killed because it was nothing but "a mass of flesh." These arguments differ from those of the eugenicists, of course, in that they are grounded in empathy—empathy that, however disingenuously expressed, makes murder acceptable. How deep does this particular sentiment run?

Toward the end of *The Life Worth Living: Disability, Pain, and Morality*, philosopher Joel Michael Reynolds recounts a family anecdote. A motorcycle-riding uncle, refusing to wear a helmet, says *I'd rather be dead than disabled*. For Reynolds, this is the folk answer to a question posed in Plato's *Crito*. On the eve of his execution, Socrates asks whether life is worth living "with a body that is corrupted and in a bad condition." Absolutely not, Crito replies. Here, at the origins of Western philosophy, is a "certainty that some forms of life are worth less than others or not worth living at all"—a certainty Reynolds traces up to the present day.

A wheelchair user myself, I've heard this sentiment—so common-sensical to some people that it doesn't register as offensive—more than once. The uncle in the anecdote, for instance, seems to have forgotten that he is in the presence of several disabled relatives, including one who uses a wheelchair. For Reynolds, his comment is revealing of a structure: by unthinkingly presuming that "disability comes along with or directly causes pain and suffering," he is making what Reynolds terms the "ableist conflation," the pernicious effects of which are traced through the book. Reynolds aims to pick this conflation apart, to show that while there are forms of pain that render life unbearable, other forms of pain are simply part of being human. There is meaningful and meaningless pain; adaptive, acute pain that can teach avoidance of fire and other hazard, and maladaptive, chronic pain that can "[evict] one from being at home in one's own body." Either of these may coincide with illness and disability, but neither are intrinsic to them. To conflate consuming, life-encompassing pain with disability, Reynolds writes, is to make a category error.

Through the ableist conflation, Reynolds makes another, more comprehensive claim: that philosophers have systematically devalued the lives of disabled people not just because of the presence of pain, but because of the absence of certain attributes. Kant believed that people with intellectual disabilities could never achieve full moral status. John Stuart Mill thought that a lack of intelligence was a priori negative, and argued that "if the fool judges their life in fact to be as satisfactory as the nonfool's, 'it is because they only know their own side of the question.'" As Reynolds points out, Mill doesn't apply the same standard to nondisabled people, who aren't required to know how life with an intellectual disability is actually experienced. The ableist conflation takes it as given that disability equals the deprivation of something quintessentially important to the good life.

This view is ultimately anchored in Aristotle, who in *Topics* defines blindness as "privation" of a "natural attribute." In *Politics*, he defines such natural attributes as essential to flourishing, to *eudaimonia*. Aristotle understood what is necessary for flourishing relative to the capacities "natural" to an adult human male, meaning that the Aristotelian candidate for *eudaimonia* is a prefiguration of the normal man—and that if you're sufficiently unlike it, no good life is possible. In other words, disability and good life are, by definition, mutually exclusive.

When faced with limits to how "useful" some people would become, eugenically minded politicians and intellectuals began to explore other options.

This doesn't quite explain, of course, why Aristotle prescribed that "no deformed child shall live." After all, he also posited that *eudaimonia* was beyond the reach of women and, as one translator of *Politics* dryly notes, while he thought that a normal female was a sort of disabled, or deformed, male, he didn't advocate universal femicide. Disabled children were a special case. If anything, Reynolds lets Aristotle off too lightly, ascribing to incompetence what can just as easily be explained by malice. Socrates and Plato get similarly kind treatments, in that they "failed to appreciate the meaning of disability." Maybe so—but maybe they understood disability perfectly well and just didn't like it very much. When Plato argued in *The Republic* that children born "deformed" should be hidden away in some "mysterious, unknown place," it was in the service of the ideal state, not the children. The context for that prescription is that people should be bred like animals, the best with the best. Even if Plato knew nothing about genetics, he had sufficiently strong opinions on heredity to sow the intellectual seeds of eugenics. And like the German racial hygienists, he didn't pretend that it would be in everyone's best interest to pursue the "improvement" of the human stock. His guardians of the state were to be as physicians to the body politic, cutting off whatever parts were damaged or diseased.

Far from a sentiment consigned to the ancients, the denigration of disability has plagued philosophy all the way through to the present day, enduring most notably, and perniciously, in modern bioethics. Peter Singer, perhaps the best-known living philosopher, provides a case in point. In his *Practical Ethics*, he notoriously endorses the euthanasia of disabled infants based on predictions about their "prospects of a worthwhile life." But why are infants with disabilities uniquely susceptible to an assessment of whether their lives are worth living? The same point comes up, too, in his infamous 2002 debates with the disability activist and lawyer Harriet McBryde Johnson, who asks him, again and again, why some forms of disability self-evidently allow for discounting a life before it has been lived. This is a matter of who gets to decide on the value of others' lives, but it is also a matter of the basis of each debater's judgment. Empirical research has repeatedly found that disabled people rate their own quality of life significantly higher than non-disabled observers predict they would, a gap wide enough that some call it the "disability paradox." But to say that this is a paradox is to presuppose that the external observer's prediction is the baseline against which the disabled person's own experience appears counter-intuitive, thus closing the logical circle.

IF YOU ASKED, you'd find that almost every disabled person—whether they were born with their impairments or acquired them later in life—does not think of themself as better off dead. The most pressing question, for them, is one familiar to any human: How should I live my life? For Reynolds, the best basis for this "project of living" is provided by social theories of disability: frameworks, put forward by activists, scholars, and allies, that view bodily differences as part of human variation, and inequitable treatment as a fault of society. This means that if there is some truth to the ableist conflation that disability aligns with privation, that is less a philosophical question than a political one. And it warns of the danger in bioethical debates that treat disability solely as a property of individuals. For example, the Canadian guidelines for aid in dying use unbearable suffering "that cannot be relieved" due to disability as a criterion of eligibility. But much of that suffering comes from other nonterminal conditions, like poverty, which can be alleviated—even if it appears intransigent under our present political conditions.

The only way out of this morass is to think about the good life as *relational*, contingent on a vision of the collective good: what Reynolds calls "worlds worth living in." The richness, variability, and pluralism of such worlds is the purview of *The Art of Flourishing*, a transcribed set of panel conversations featuring disabled scholars, educators, artists, and activists who make meaning in their lives not in embodied isolation or according to any single standard, but in relation with other human beings and the material world, according to their subjective point of view. Contra Aristotelian *eudaimonia*, an objective measure grounded in a particular physiological and social standard, the editors argue that "the authority for determining what specific capacities are required for life to be meaningful or enjoyable should lie with disabled people themselves."

The panelists share no single "deficit," but a series of overlapping experiences that involve both their bodies and their relationships with technology, medicine, community-building, the articulation of a sustainable identity, and creativity. Ludwig Wittgenstein called these sorts of category structures "family resemblances." He gave games as an example: while a tabletop game may not have a rectangular board or involve rolling dice, it can still be a fully-fledged member of the category. That seems about right for disability. People with mobility impairments have little in common with people with visual impairments, intellectual disabilities, or chronic pain, except that they do: a resemblance not in any single shared deficit, but in the resonance between distinct experiences of not fitting in. Disabled lives ought to be compared, both to each other and to non-disabled lives, but never hierarchized, subject to a central normative standard.

One of the editors of the anthology, Rosemarie Garland-Thomson, coined the term "normate" to describe how the average human being became both an empirical standard of measurement and an aspirational ideal. One of the fathers of modern statistics, Adolphe Quetelet, explicitly argued that *l'homme moyen*, the "average man" should set the aesthetic as well as moral standard for society. That has become the reality in many fields, as what we understand as problematically "abnormal" isn't necessarily harmful or dangerous, only sufficiently far from the center of the bell curve. Height is one example: in the postwar period, a considerable number of young women were prescribed growth-suppressing drugs not for medical reasons, but on the expectation that they would grow unusually tall and therefore have trouble "fitting in."

The notion of the good life has not just been an ideal to strive for. It has also been a criterion for identifying lives that are not worthy.

By definition, of course, the average excludes much of humanity. Whether disabled or non-disabled, many of us are not normal. The difference, though, is that disability is a condition whereby normality cannot even be pretended to. Once again, disability is disavowed through a form of circular logic: The bounds of normality end where disability begins, and disability is defined as whatever form of embodiment that precludes a normal life. It's precisely this quality that makes disability a concept that can serve a liberatory function. Maybe, in its incompatibility with normality—and to the philosophical conceptions of the good life tethered to it—disability can be conducive to a new, pluralistic conception of flourishing. In *The Art of Flourishing*, the panelists explore this pluralism by reckoning with their own bodies. In one panel, the activist Yomi Young, who has osteogenesis imperfecta, speaks of abandoning walking, with the risk of falls and fractures, in favor of the "exoskeleton" of her wheelchair. "When it comes to trying to approximate able-bodiedness," she tells her interlocutors, "I have no interest." It is the kind of tradeoff that many disabled people make, but crucially, it isn't that different from tradeoffs that others make, too—between risks and benefits, comfort and stigma. Young's just entails a clearer break with the unsupported assumption that walking is something required for a full human life. The book's central point of reference is the work of the late activist and MacArthur fellow Alice Wong, whose decade-long project Disability Visibility—the name both a description of its work and something of a rallying cry—published stories, art, and essays documenting what it means to live in a non-standard body in a world that is hostile to them. Disability Visibility features lives lived under siege, but also lives lived well: a multitude of demonstrations of just how broad a range human flourishing can encompass.

Socrates may have discounted corrupted bodies, but he also extolled the importance of knowing yourself. For *The Art of Flourishing*, perhaps the richest arguments against the deficit model emerge from its evocation of disability as a creative force, closely related to art and attentiveness to the relationship between embodiment and how we experience the world. Art, of course, is intrinsically pluralistic: while there is at any given time a richest human being on the planet, there is no greatest living artist—nor could there be, so long as art encompasses different genres, traditions, modes of expression, and aesthetic ideals.

In one example, the rabbi and scholar Julia Watts Belser recounts her collaboration with the choreographer Claire Cunningham, who uses crutches and "describes herself as a four-footed creature, one who loves to explore rocky places, to probe those nooks and crannies." The resulting piece, *We Run Like Rivers*, is a series of short audio works that combine music with verbal description of the subtleties of nonstandard mobility, whether walking with crutches or rolling in wheelchairs, across different types of terrain. It is an exploration of disability as something that forces and facilitates attention to place: to the material world, and who we are in it, but also a rejection of unaided walking as the standard against which everything else should be measured. The image of the river is a good way to capture the flowlike experience of wheelchair motion; as fast as or slightly faster than walking, but still slow enough to fully take in the landscape as one moves, continuously and without the slight sense of disconnect as one foot and then another leaves the ground. One way of moving isn't a priori better than the other, and can't serve as the other's standard: they're simply different.

In another piece, Georgina Kleege, a scholar of visual impairment and visual art, recounts her practice of bringing blindness into the museum. For her, the Richard Serra sculpture *Sequence*, sixty-seven feet long and built out of ship-grade waterproof steel, isn't only a haptic object, something to touch, but a sonic object, big enough to become a distinct aural environment, to be explored through shouts, taps, and reverberations. *Deprived of sight* is still something you could say about Kleege, but it would be the least interesting possible way to describe her.

THE CONVERSATIONS TRANSCRIBED in *The Art of Flourishing* were hosted by the Hastings Center, a bioethical research institute, and the book bears an explicitly normative frame. To be sure, the editors' call for more supportive environments for human beings of every kind of embodiment is a utopian ideal, particularly in a time when disability rights are in retreat in many countries (most saliently the United States), and when data science and advanced genetics are facilitating radical new methods for determining which kinds of people will enter the world. Where prenatal diagnostics used to be a matter of identifying single-gene diseases, startups like Nucleus are now selling the promise of using polygenic patterns to determine a wide range of traits in the next generation. The ideal being promoted is one of optimization: smarter, taller, thinner, fitter. But just what are we doing all this optimizing *for*?

This ideology's nineteenth- and twentieth-century predecessors were mostly organized around the negative pole, the aim of preventing "inferior" people from reproducing, because even its proponents knew that they had no reliable tools for securing the reproduction and refinement of "superior" qualities. Today, with forced sterilization largely off the table (though not entirely, particularly when it comes to women with intellectual disabilities), the new eugenics accentuates the positive. Its most radical sect, transhumanism, aims to improve human health, intelligence, and other capacities until there emerges a literal new species with none of the problems of the old one. But classical eugenics, too, fed on comparable fantasies of utopian improvement, on the dream of perfecting Man, whether in a universal form or in the more specific shape of the master race. That fantasy is inextricable from the fears of degeneration and miscegenation, precisely because true perfection is necessarily unattainable in this imperfect world; eugenics-adjacent techno-utopians like Musk seem unable to complete a paragraph about the glorious future without warning about imminent catastrophe. But so long as the deficits and shortcomings can be projected onto others, the utopian vision can survive.

It isn't news that the aspiring philosopher-kings of Silicon Valley view the good life in the singular. Some of them, most prominently Ray Kurzweil, the futurist hailed for his ostensibly oracular gifts of prediction, dream of the Singularity, a time in the near future where artificial general intelligence, or superintelligence, becomes real—at which point humans will merge with this nascent supreme being or else become obsolete. Kurzweil gestures vaguely at the possibility of curing all illnesses and rectifying all disabilities, but mostly as proofs of concept. The real point, for him, is to achieve transcendent perfection. Those who cannot merge, those who lack the cognitive or economic resources to upgrade, or simply don't have the right hardware to begin with, will necessarily fall short of this ideal. If anything, the new dispensation treats more of humanity than ever as useless eaters.

Disabled people are uniquely positioned to question the near-universal standards that orient life toward productivity and output.

In the face of this, what will it take for disabled people to be acknowledged as fully human beings—to escape the oubliette of Plato's "mysterious, unknown place"? For starters, to reject the idea that the body is a machine built for productivity, and that humans can be obsolete, a troubling concept that evokes the long history of cultural evolutionism, where some peoples are, essentially, consigned to the scrapheap of history. Next, to abandon the dizzying heights of *the* good life, the place where the human species is conflated with a singular ideal, and to come down to earth, where good lives are oriented to, and derive from, meaning-making in the company of other human beings. Yomi Young notes the cultural stereotype that people with her condition are unusually intelligent, then explains that, no, her physical fragility was an early impetus toward learning how to communicate as precisely as possible. On the singular reading, intelligence is a saving grace, a compensation for a deficit and something to put to work. On the relational reading, variation in embodiment and needs drives us to interact with others, drives complexity, and makes for a richer world.

This kind of living, I think, has normative implications beyond the remit of the self-identified disabled. As a rejection of the near-universal standards that orient life toward productivity and output, it challenges us to ask what we actually want to do with our time on the planet—a question in dire need of asking as Silicon Valley simultaneously promises to increase productivity beyond measure and threatens to create mass unemployment in white-collar industries. I am an academic with a modest research budget; there is nothing to prevent me, for instance, from employing dozens of AI agents to generate dozens of papers for me, using my human skills to supervise and edit the "writing." It's just not what I think of as flourishing.

Disabled people are uniquely positioned to make this critique because the game of productivity is one we can never really win. Not only are we structurally disadvantaged; if we do well enough, we no longer count as *really* disabled. The category of disability is unstable, irreducible to the biological attributes of individuals; it speaks to marginalization that shifts with time and place. In different ways and to different degrees, human societies have had a need to disavow the qualities of our humanity that people find most painful to confront: that we are vulnerable, mortal, and dependent on others to survive. It is comfortable, perhaps, to keep such qualities at arm's length by projecting them onto a minority and excluding its members. But since anyone can join this minority at any time through illness or injury, it is also necessary to believe some individuals can overcome the barriers that society has created, if only they align sufficiently with its values. Disability, then, reveals not only what lives society thinks unworthy of life, but what it thinks of all of us.

The productivity game doesn't appear to be going away any time soon, but despite the technophilic fantasies to the contrary, disability isn't going away, either. Besides the fact that genetics is a lot more complicated than the ads for Nucleus Genomics pretend, millions of people become disabled every year from accidents and acquired illnesses, not to mention from violence and war—something that should neither be celebrated nor ignored. Instead, we should ameliorate disability marginalization as best we can, through measures that are far more robust and well-proven than eugenic experimentation: public health, peace work, and welfare state capacity building, for starters. Making a better world is hard, but to abandon that effort in favor of making better people seems a way to ensure that the good life, for all but an anointed few, will remain perpetually out of reach. **BR**

THE MACHINES GET IN THE WAY

Luke Dunne

Your Name Here
Helen DeWitt and Ilya Gridneff
Dalkey Archive Press, 2025

NOWHERE IS LABOR'S INVISIBILITY more highly prized than in the production of fiction. On the one hand, writers remain the principal landmarks for navigating the literary landscape, dominating its psychogeography far more than aesthetic movements or national literatures: we are, in the main, readers and enthusiasts of Proust, not of modernism or French literature per se. On the other hand, our aesthetic appraisals largely valorize the writer's self-erasure. Realism, which in spite of everything remains the dominant mode of "literary fiction," all but requires this.

More recent developments—autofiction among them—have nothing on this most successful innovation in the history of the novel. From the original, nineteenth-century form popularized by Balzac, Zola, and Stendhal to the "lyrical" variant of today, the verisimilitude that realism pursues—not just lifelikeness, but worldlikeness—is meant to convince us the novel is, for want of a better term, natural. The writer, to say nothing of agents, publishers, editors, and the rest, must be kept off stage; their presence would be fatal for what Tom Wolfe called "the 'absorbing' or the 'gripping' quality that is peculiar to the novel." Happy though we are to bring the magicians out from behind the curtain once the trick is done—when the author's labor often becomes a text's competitive advantage, its unique selling proposition, and as such must be aggressively publicized—we seem still to prefer, in the moment of reading, not to know how, exactly, they did it.

Your Name Here, a novel cowritten by Helen DeWitt and Ilya Gridneff, tells us how they did it. An unusually ingenious attempt to represent the way a work of fiction comes to be, or fails to, the book follows its two authors—sometimes wearing fictional disguises, sometimes not—as they attempt to get a novel, this novel, into print. In this, it takes its place in a long line of satires of publishing, from R. F. Kuang's *Yellowface* (2023) and Percival Everett's *Erasure* (2001) all the way back to George Gissing's *New Grub Street* (1891), while pushing the genre to more adventurous formal extremes. Written in the mid-2000s but published only last year, it is a novel about writing, yes, but it is also a novel about everything that gets in the way of it: appeasing editors, wooing agents, making (and breaking) contracts, and all the other dirty, discouraging work required to get the literary sausage into its casing, unfolding against the backdrop of a society being scrambled by new technology and ever-intensifying pressures of self-branding and self-promotion.

The book's centerpiece is the email correspondence between DeWitt and Gridneff, complete with ubiquitous misspellings (which I won't be *sic*-ing) and banner ads for long-since discontinued digital products ("Be the first to hear what's new at MSN—sign up to our free newsletters!"). Their e-pistolary is frequently interrupted by a dizzying kaleidoscope of other genres, scenes, and personae, among them anecdotes from Gridneff's life as a tabloid journalist; part-novels written by DeWitt/her avatars (the longest is called *Lotteryland*, a trenchant satire of Blairite Britain); and ongoing attempts to teach the reader Arabic, accompanied by charming if overearnest speculations about the good that could be achieved, geopolitically speaking, if a novel somehow managed to smuggle Middle Eastern languages into their pages, as Tolkien did with the tongues of Middle Earth.

This is a recipe for some good, clean, postmodern fun, propelled along by the interplay of Gridneff's singular voice—charismatic, vulgar, deranged—and DeWitt's contrapuntal polyphonies. It coheres into that rare thing, a six-hundred-page novel that one does not finish with a sense of relief. Along the way, we get an eccentric yet moving portrait of the work of art—and the work of making art—in an age that feels ever more hostile to it.

Gridneff's relationship with DeWitt evolves slowly, from a sloppy first meeting at a bar ("met a woman whose name escapes but described herself as a novelist and I discuss Ardorno having never read any of his texts"), through the writing process (including frequent pleas, on Gridneff's part, for emergency loans until the advance comes in), up until the crushing realization that the novel just isn't going to get published (except, of course, it is). It often makes for a frustrating read, not only because some of the obstacles DeWitt and Gridneff face are truly infuriating but because others seem eminently navigable. Even a sympathetic reader may catch themselves asking, *why can't you pick up the telephone, or write a friendly email, or just be nicer to people?*

Making art while making a living, connecting as opposed to transacting with the world: both have become harder, and harder than they have to be.

Equally futile questions are often posed to those suffering from depression, and the similarity isn't incidental. Large portions of the book find DeWitt in a kind of fugue state, either contemplating suicide or, at several points, attempting it. "I came to Berlin partly because someone once recommended KaDeWe as a suicide spot and partly because I thought I should not be at large with a gun," she tells Gridneff at one point. Elsewhere: "had a bad time in ny with my publishers, tried suicide by a method that didn't work, went to niagara falls (banal i know). did not realise instructions to my publishers' lawyer constituted a press release. kafkaesque experience at nf psychiatric ward, sort of like a book tour only with a kosher mini-breakfast."

DeWitt has long been forthright about this. As she told *The Believer* in 2012, "I point to the breakdowns, the clinical depression, the suicide attempts—and it never makes any difference. . . . I put clauses in my contracts and I explain: this clause stands between me and suicide, don't sign this contract if you are not going to comply with it—and they laugh." It's easy enough—too easy—to dismiss this as emotional blackmail. People can be difficult, in the art world as in all things: that's the human side of literary production that realism prefers to obscure. If instead you hear only entitlement, it's worth recalling literary critic Mark McGurl's observation, in *The Novel Art* (2001), that "the vicious snobbery one frequently encounters in and around modernism is, if one cares to look closely, a complex phenomenon manifesting both an injured sense of aristocratic entitlement and, at times, a strenuous attempt to resist, so as to mediate, the naked force of capital on behalf of other values." Something similar is going on in *Your Name Here*. The question the novel invites us to ask is not why DeWitt or any other writer can't just play the game but why, exactly, they're expected to.

One answer—the one the novel leans most heavily toward—is that people who work in publishing and media more generally are stupid and mendacious, prone to miscommunications, changes of tack, and incompetence of the sort that DeWitt and Gridneff document at length. That's an age-old complaint, and certainly there's plenty of it around. Less visible in the novel is literary publishing's ever-dwindling resources and cultural importance. How do you sell books and keep a press financially afloat in the twenty-first century? What can publishers and editors reasonably *do* to capture readers' scarce attention? Such matters are addressed only fleetingly in *Your Name Here*, but its limited value as diagnosis doesn't diminish it as a novel. Indeed, though it presents as a pessimistic take on the publishing industry, I found myself reading it against the grain: there is something almost optimistic about attending to mutable human failings rather than the inexorable victory of market forces.

In any case, if things are even half as bad as depicted in *Your Name Here* for writers of DeWitt's standing, so much the worse for the rest of us. Her work has been near-universally acclaimed, and her first novel, *The Last Samurai* (2000), is frequently cited among the best of this century. Yet being published by an indie press, even a prestigious one like New Directions (DeWitt's usual publisher), doesn't come close to paying the bills. In April, DeWitt revealed that Yale's Windham-Campbell Prize—founded with the respectable aim of giving writers "the opportunity to focus on their work independent of financial concerns"—intended to award her $175,000, but the grant was conditioned on promotional obligations DeWitt said she was not able to fulfill.

Ironically, Gridneff recalls their collaboration beginning with "a simple, even misguided, motive: to make a quick buck. Helen hoped it would launch my writing career and free me from the tabloid world that was funding my nomadic life." Instead, their book was stalled for eighteen (eighteen!) years in the literary equivalent of development hell (the novel doesn't name names, but DeWitt has told the story at length on her blog); in the meantime, DeWitt posted the book on her website alongside a request for donations. The delay, though doubtless stressful for its authors, is oddly fitting, since it's easier to read *Your Name Here* as the variant of the historical novel it is—an end-of-historical novel?—now that the period it describes is in the past. The book turns the conditions of its making into a prism, refracting the strange world we've inherited from the mid-to-late aughts.

THE MANY METAFICTIONS and intertexts make *Your Name Here* an unusual hybrid: at once a maximalist, neo-modernist novel in the tradition of David Foster Wallace, Thomas Pynchon, and William H. Gass and a historical novel of a deceptively traditional kind. György Lukács's definition of the latter remains the industry standard; as Perry Anderson summarizes it: "an epic depicting a transformation of popular life through a set of representative human types whose lives are reshaped by sweeping social forces. Famous historical figures will feature among the dramatis personae, but their roles in the tale will be oblique or marginal."

Your Name Here is certainly epic in scope, a function both of the part-novels with their various locales and Gridneff's relentless globe-trotting, from London to Berlin to Kurdistan to Russia and back again (doing "dirty deeds as a papparazzi writer"). Though none of this constitutes a traditional epic voyage, Gridneff appears as a kind of immature Odysseus: crafty and periodically duplicitous, but not ready to return to Ithaca just yet. As for "famous historical figures" with roles "oblique or marginal," well, Gridneff's missives from the frontlines of tabloid journalism serve them up aplenty:

> I am not in London any more, was sent to Santorini, Greece, popular island, for . . . Angelina Jolie and Bread Shitt, (not being there) and decided not to return.
>
> [...]
>
> There are the big names—there are always the big names—but what happens is they are flooded with crap stories. Even so, you can sometimes surprise them with a new angle. Jennifer Aniston's brother,

for instance, there is probably some material there.

[...]

returned to London to be sent away by Amerika's National Enquirer magazine- yes to work for an organ of such hyperreality is a dream come true! Indeed, to chase Britney Spears around Europe- hit me baby one more time - to have her simulation pay for my move to Berlin, eat sauerkraut and worst with the money i EARNT from her gyriating virgin whore vagina image -the black (w)hole - lived there for six months- wrote READ drank koffee then realised berlin was ... not for me///

Then there's the "transformation of popular life" by "sweeping social forces," most notably the birth of digital culture and its new forms of consumerism and celebrity. Despite hailing from the "old internet" of blogs and email, *Your Name Here* prefigures the new, now increasingly enshittified internet with eerie prescience. Gridneff's very existence seems to foreshadow the delirium of the newsfeed—he's broadcasting from all over the world, punning and memeing with staggering fluency, mingling light pornography and celebrity gossip with theoryspeak and serious reportage. A baffling carousel of low-quality images bookending certain chapters seems to adhere to its own meme-logic; we get grainy stills of Adorno, Terry Gilliam, Marcello Mastroianni, and Jessica Rabbit (yes, the "sexy" cartoon bunny)—like reading Sebald, but if he were on bath salts.

But *Your Name Here* is not, or not only, an autofictional internet novel *avant le lettre*. In the background are imperialist ventures in the Middle East, the degeneration of news media into entertainment, the corrosion of civil society, spiraling income inequality and state surveillance. Like a foul-mouthed, hyperarticulate Barry Lyndon or Forrest Gump, Gridneff has a knack for arriving on the scene at the very moment that the historical conjuncture becomes most threatening while somehow escaping intact:

I am actually in Iraq right now=-not kopf kutting off territory but a zone creating enough sense not to stay the night here- despite several offers. heads begin falling below Mosul- so they say. once again hoping to get published- a story something like one day in iraq...

Lotteryland, meanwhile, excoriates the blandness and banality of turn-of-the-century neoliberalism. One of its more prominent dystopian features is the enforced exposure to a suspiciously Blair-like form of govspeak, blared into households at all hours of the day: *"You know, there are lots of prizes for everyone. Sometimes we win and sometimes we lose. Sometimes it's easy to dwell on the prizes we haven't won. It's easy to feel unlucky if we don't win. But remember, no matter what you win, no matter what you don't win, you're still you. And that's an incredibly special person to be..."*

Given all this, it's probably unsurprising that DeWitt has claimed the following words, spoken by Foster Wallace in a 1997 TV interview, encapsulate "everything I might have wanted to say about life, the universe, postmodernism and *Your Name Here*":

> There's a way, it seems to me, that reality's fractured right now, at least the reality that I live in. The difficulty about . . . writing about that reality is that text is very linear and it's very unified. . . . I, anyway, am constantly on the lookout for ways to fracture the text that aren't totally disorienting. I mean, you can take the lines and jumble them up and that's nicely fractured, but nobody's gonna read it.

Some will say DeWitt and Gridneff should have taken this advice—fracture the text by all means, but don't totally disorient the reader. Yet they do just enough. The result is more *Ulysses* than *Finnegans Wake*: digressive but not entirely disintegrated.

It's here the novel shows its age, with poignant results. The idea that writers should have something to say about the "fracturing" of reality may be the central conceit of our era, but so too is the notion that reality is *too* fractured to permit simple mimesis between work and world. In *Free Indirect: The Novel in a Postfictional Age* (2022), Timothy Bewes finds that the "insistent quality" in the work of so many contemporary novelists—Rachel Cusk, Ben Lerner, Teju Cole, Zadie Smith—is "not only refusing to connect the work and the world but of thinking, inhabiting, even forging the space of their disconnection." *Your Name Here* tries to connect: to represent disintegration rather than the impossibility of doing so.

Ditto in the realm of character, which Bewes sees as ground zero for disconnection. "I'm not interested in character because I don't think character exists anymore," Cusk has said. If that's true, it's easy to understand why writers of her generation are inclined to erode the distinction between a fictional person and a real one, but *Your Name Here* does the opposite, sharpening it at every opportunity. Figures change names frequently and without warning; hundreds of bit players appear only for a sentence or two. Character hasn't dissolved here, but neither has it reverted to Forsterian "roundness" in the conventional wisdom of the creative writing workshop. Instead, character functions as a challenge, an obstacle to easy reading and ready comprehension, and hence to the "immediacy" that Anna Kornbluh has identified as the characteristic literary style of "too late capitalism." Difficulty as disruptor of immediacy, mediation with a human face: here again, the novel shows its modernist inheritance.

As the prospect of publishing peters out, the authors start to resent one another. In the real world, difficulties—with money and in relationships—aren't always so easily resolved.

"It seemed to me," DeWitt has said, "that the speakers in Plato and Thucydides were more real as characters than what we think of as 'fleshed-out characters'—those with physical descriptions and personal histories—because their style of argument establishes how they engage with the world." In *Your Name Here*, the terms of engagement are ultimately financial, rendering the distinction between fictional and nonfictional its most painfully obvious. Fictional characters—those contained in the part-novels—tend to find ingenious solutions to their money woes. DeWitt and Gridneff, meanwhile, remain stuck. The prospect of publishing peters out, and the authors start to resent one another. In the real world, difficulties—with money and in relationships—aren't always so easily resolved.

OF COURSE, THE NOVEL did, eventually, get published—by Dalkey Archive, now a Deep Vellum imprint, one of the largest publishers with an explicitly experimental and non-commercial bent. But one gets the sense that this isn't the book *Your Name Here* was meant to be, as DeWitt herself has admitted. "The half of the book that was to be my contribution had less and less to do with what I wanted to write," she told *The Believer*. "Meanwhile, I was sending it out, engaging with agents, transacting with the world—manically hustling when I wanted to finish other books. This would never have been great, but it was harder to bear given that the final version was not the kind of text I had envisaged."

To dismiss this kind of talk as the tiresome expression of writerly perfectionism or the banal failure of an idea to pan out is exactly the kind of thinking *Your Name Here* tries to jolt us out of. If the novel only partially succeeds, it also convincingly refutes a strictly aesthetic understanding of its limitations. Making art while making a living, connecting as opposed to transacting with the world: both have become harder, and harder than they have to be. Sometimes artistic failures are systemic failures; sometimes, as one of DeWitt's surrogates puts it, "I know what I want to do but the machines get in the way." **BR**

A still from Kelly Reichardt's *The Mastermind*. Image: Mubi

ART THIEVES

Jacob Rubin

The Mastermind
directed by Kelly Reichardt
filmscience and Mubi, 2025

IN KELLY REICHARDT'S LATEST FILM, *The Mastermind*, the scheme of James Blaine "J. B." Mooney (Josh O'Connor) to extract four Arthur Dove paintings from the Framingham Museum of Art gets off to a rather poor start. On the day of the heist, an October morning in 1970, class is out for a teacher's workday, a fact Mooney, an unemployed carpenter, discovers when he arrives at the school with his two boys in tow. Forced to improvise, he deposits the children at a local bowling alley, near where he is to meet his getaway driver, anyway. Moments later this jumpy underling pulls up with the stolen wheels, fingers the envelope of cash Mooney hands him, and ducks into another suddenly appearing vehicle. "This is real shitty, man," Mooney yells as the car backs away. "Real shitty!"

After the robbery has begun in earnest, things don't improve much. One of J. B.'s two henchmen flashes a gun at a schoolgirl in the museum, tussles with a security guard, and, once outside, pulls the weapon on the schoolgirl's friends, whose car is blocking the circular driveway the crew needs to escape from. This loose cannon will, in a matter of days, be arrested for a bank robbery and rat Mooney out to the police. When this news hits the local paper, the last of Mooney's partners demands a meet-up outside of town where a crew of mobsters ambush the thief and toss him into their car. Wedged in the back, J. B. wears the fidgety, self-righteous air of a scolded child. "I don't think you thought things through enough," the thuggish driver offers as his colleagues, in the back of the frame, load the Doves into the trunk, fishing them out of the barn where Mooney has stowed them. An hour into the movie, the jig is already up.

The droll speed with which Mooney's plot is foiled is but one of the many ways Reichardt upends the conventions of the heist film.

Reichardt's finely plotted films, despite their slowness and open-endedness, are often gripping examples of genre as much as they are deconstructions of it; she works like a canny jazz soloist who, in order to play around the downbeat, must know exactly where it falls. In *First Cow* and *Meek's Cutoff*, she subverts the white masculinist strain in the Western by centering, in the first film, a gentle cook and a Chinese immigrant who open a pop-up bakery in an 1820 mining town, and in the second, a strong-willed wife who misplaces her trust in a Native American captive her lost party of settlers has taken hostage. *Wendy and Lucy*, which follows a young woman from Indiana heading to Alaska to find work during the Great Recession, is a road-trip movie in which the car breaks down at the start of the film. *River of Grass*, the filmmaker's debut, depicts the fugitive wanderings of a loser named Lee and a dissatisfied housewife, Cozy, who must go on the lam after they believe—incorrectly, it later turns out—they've shot and killed a man whose backyard pool they've crashed.

In *The Mastermind*, the droll speed with which Mooney's plot is foiled is but one of the many ways Reichardt upends the conventions of the heist film. In contrast to the cat-burglar elegance that typify the genre, the Framingham rip is laughably clumsy, a near smash and grab. Fecklessness and betrayal have hollowed out the game camaraderie the band of criminals usually share. Most jarring of all, it's never explicitly clear why J. B. hatches his boneheaded plot in the first place.

One likely motive is boredom. The film opens with the art school dropout standing apart from his sons and wife as they tour the museum. He seems distracted and moments later lifts a figurine of a soldier from a glass cabinet, slipping it into his glasses case. At a deadening dinner with his parents, he is needled by his self-important father, a circuit county judge, for not having done as well as a peer named Kip, who runs his own outfit. Mooney asserts that Kip is an inferior carpenter and that he himself has no interest in being a manager. A few scenes later Mooney cons his mother out of the seed money for his criminal venture by pretending an architect has commissioned him to install Japanese-style cabinetry in a refurbished house in the tony end of town (he needs funds for a workspace and tools, he tells her). The cruel pretense seems a bitter commentary on the life that would be expected of him, or the one he might one day have to resign himself to.

A material clue, though, is dropped later in the film. After ditching his wife and kids to evade the cops, Mooney holes up with an old buddy, Fred, and his partner, Maude, in their farmhouse in what is maybe upstate New York. Fred, like a fawning nephew, reads aloud from an article about Mooney, now a bona fide fugitive. "No more chipping away at the edges, huh?" he says. "This time you've blown it all up!" Maude is less charmed. Her glare could burn a hole through Mooney, and, in a late-night tête-à-tête, after J. B. has taken the last beer in the fridge, she commands him to leave. An intimate gesture seems to suggest the two had once slept together, and that Mooney might try to seduce her. But she isn't having it. A Dove painting hung in the office of Professor Pruitt, Mooney's thesis advisor in art school, Maude says. "He was your fence," she asserts.

O'Connor's expression, faced with this accusation, is warmly, reflexively gaslight-y. Earlier in the film, the would-be getaway driver asks, "How exactly do the paintings get spun into cash?" "You keep asking me that," Mooney says. "You keep not answering," the driver replies. "Because . . . you don't need to know," Mooney says. A flit of concern sails through the fog of his self-satisfaction, like a small bird, and disappears again.

Maude's theory is never confirmed one way or another, and Pruitt never appears. Mooney does enjoy a full free day between the completion of the robbery and the appearance of law enforcement officers in his home, and he seems to be in no rush to contact anyone. On that afternoon, rather, after his wife and kids have cleared out, he hangs one of the paintings above the couch in his living room and admires it, with a look of spent labor, something even close to awe. Is he meant to resemble an artist gazing upon their finished work? Was something like this moment, this cosplaying as a creator, his reward?

REICHARDT GREW UP in Miami, with an undercover narcotics agent mother and a crime-scene technician father, and many of her films hinge on criminal acts. In *Night Moves*, ecoterrorists blow up the Peter Green Dam in Oregon, accidentally killing a man who was camping nearby. In *Wendy and Lucy*, Wendy is arrested and fatefully parted from her beloved dog after shoplifting pet food from a supermarket. The plucky bakers in *First Cow* illegally milk Chief Factor's cow at night. And the outlaws of *River of Grass*, despite their initial misapprehension, end up committing a slew of petty crimes, and a last, fatal one; Lee lifts clothes from a laundromat and booze from a liquor store, and is later shot and killed by Cozy.

Reichardt has cited as an influence Ursula K. Le Guin's essay "The Carrier Bag Theory of Fiction," in which the science-fiction writer presents a narrative theory inspired by Elizabeth Fisher's *Women's Creation*. The ur-technological breakthrough of our species, Fisher wrote, was not a carved bone to bash an enemy's head or an arrow to pierce their flesh, but a "recipient . . . some kind of sling or net," a bag to hold berries, leaves, sprouts, and roots. Riffing on this idea, Le Guin presents a counter-metaphor for fiction. Stories, she contends, need not be akin to weapons and the heroic, linear conflicts in which they are put to use; they can, rather, resemble giant totes full of jumbled, jostling items. And if the story is a bag, the storyteller is the person who collects and curates what goes inside.

For Le Guin, the myth of Prometheus is an exemplar of the opposing and dominant narrative template, that of a masculinist or tragic-heroic bent, the kind that centers the glory and tragedy of the hunt. Each metaphor—the Promethean and the carrier bag—suggests a distinct image for a criminal. In the first, the lawless figure is a fitting symbol for the artist, both being glamorous iconoclasts who run afoul of bourgeois norms and answer to their own audacious desires. And in many great crime films that tacitly adhere to the Promethean premise, the crook is, indeed, very cool, shot through with dark passions that run parallel to the director's own. Michel, the anti-hero of Bresson's *Pickpocket*, embodies a searching intensity that marks the film as a whole. The old-world manner and familial concerns of Don Corleone echo the chiaroscuro and drawing-room ensembles Coppola decorates *The Godfather* with. *Goodfellas*'s Henry Hill, addicted to the flashy lifestyle of the gangster, is a mirror for Scorsese, who harbors a parallel avidity for the sensuality of cinema itself.

In *The Mastermind*, though, there is nothing remotely cool about being a criminal. I kept expecting Mooney's luck to turn around, for him to flee the country or come back to his family, or to somehow recover the paintings, imagining the movie would make good on a tacit Promethean promise. But like Cervantes' knight-errant, it's all windmills for the poor bastard. After being banished by Maude, J. B. drifts among the boarding houses of Ohio, marked by kitschy cat art and views of brick walls. His wife hangs up on him when he calls for a much-needed cash infusion. Donning an ill-fitting gray suit he lifted from the closet of a rented room, he resembles more and more what he is—a homeless man, witnessing, with bewilderment, the passing vignettes of those who still enjoy society's embrace: a naval cadet gently setting his Dixie cup on his infant's head; a couple at a picnic; two boys standing on a rusted car throwing rocks into a river. In the film's closing sequence, and in an ugly echo of his prior shakedown of his mother, the desperate crook mugs an old lady, rushes off with her purse, and ducks into an anti–Vietnam War protest where he is mistaken for an activist and thrown in a paddy wagon by the Cincinnati police.

Here we have a film that makes the life of crime seem completely shitty and lonely—not because the filmmaker has set out to send a message or pass moral judgment, but because her art, I think, authentically subscribes to the kind of worldview that is evoked by Le Guin's image of the carrier bag. "Science fiction properly conceived, like all serious fiction," Le Guin writes in the same essay, "is a way of trying to describe what is in fact going on, what people actually do and feel, how people relate to everything else in this vast sack, this belly of the universe." In this philosophy the criminal, a figure whose transgressive behavior irrevocably separates them from most others, lives in a state of terminal confusion about where they are and what is around them, pushing again and again the meshing that holds them and everyone else. A creature like that is less likely to be a daring individualist than a lost soul who is down and out or a spiritually indigent creep who is contemptuous and paranoid. With the exception of the daring bakers in *First Cow* (who steal the milk to a generous, if profiteering, end) and a remorseful co-conspirator, played by Dakota Fanning, in *Night Moves*, a pathetic air hangs over all who break the law in Reichardt's filmography.

IF A CRIMINAL IS not an apt symbol for the artist in Reichardt's work, what is? In *Showing Up*, Reichardt follows the passive-aggressive friendship between two artists, the more freewheeling and expansive Jo (Hong Chau) and the irritated and bedraggled sculptor Lizzy (Michelle Williams). Jo is Lizzy's landlord and has left Lizzy without hot water for two weeks. Lizzy works in the administrative office of a local art college, where she is hardly recognized as an artist in her own right. Her divorced parents use her as a go-between for their ongoing spats, and her mentally disturbed brother has little capacity to pay attention to her. Lizzy is hardly sexy or even happy, but she is crankily incorruptible and capable of tender devotion, even sorcery. In one scene, she removes, with an apology, an arm from a small clay girl she's working on; when she affixes a new limb, the piece glows with a sudden majesty.

Reichardt captures this same aura of unassuming magic and quiet immersion in two short documentaries of sculptors at work (both can be streamed on the Criterion Channel). One of them, "Bronx, New York, November 2019," follows Michelle Segre for a day in her studio; the other, "Cal State Long Beach, CA, January 2020" records Jessica Jackson Hutchins and Alexander Demetriou. Segre, wearing a utility glove, threads a needle through a giant black kite-like thing. Demetriou slaps and shapes big blocks of clay, like a pizza maker. Hutchins smoothes her paint-covered hand over the cracks in a bulbous ceramic work. In the first of these films, Reichardt now and then cuts to an elevated train rattling across the Bronx or to men hosing trucks in a carwash, seeming to indicate that the artist, while doing something special that is worth filming, is contiguous with other vital curiosities. It is as if Segre is an item in a big bag of the city while fashioning her own in the sanctity of the studio.

Mooney hangs one of the paintings above the couch in his living room and admires it, with a look of spent labor, something even close to awe. Is he meant to resemble an artist gazing upon their finished work?

This dual citizenship of the artist—having one foot in our world and one in the universe of their own creation—is what is so moving and subtly subversive about the portrait of Lizzy in *Showing Up*. She is a regular Joe with out-to-lunch parents and a tiring day job who also, on occasion, practices beautiful and transformative rites in her studio-garage. A criminal would not be a coherent image for such an ignorable but serious laborer with intelligent hands. A gentle handyman, maybe, or an acupuncturist, or, in loftier terms, one of Shelley's "unacknowledged legislators."

And poor J. B.—what is he? In *The Mastermind*, there are a couple glimpses of an artist lurking inside the failed thief. Mooney has rendered painstaking color illustrations of the paintings to be taken, distributing them to his henchman as they roll up to the museum. And there is a hypnotic six-minute sequence of J. B. unloading the Doves from a homemade wooden container into the loft of the barn, in the dark of night, alone. But these flashes of skill and attentive labor answer to a different priority. They serve only taking, the removing of art he seems to admire from a space where others could see it. Like many destructive and unhappy people, he is close to being an artist and yet very far from becoming one. Having internalized the worst emphases of the Promethean premise, he finds himself in a carrier-bag world.

Mooney is someone we've all encountered our fair share of: fatal sufferers of main character syndrome who, below a layer or two of charisma, are nothing more than mooches and takers. But, as I thought about the film, another association came to mind. In his beautiful study *The Gift*, Lewis Hyde explains the etymology of an "Indian giver." The epithet now describes someone who demands the return of a present. But the term, he writes, was originally used by colonists to characterize Native Americans, who, when offering a pipe, expected it to be returned—a logic still so foreign to our Western sensibility that Hyde is moved to slander its antipode. "The opposite of an 'Indian giver,' [in this original sense]" Hyde writes, "would be something like 'white man keeper' (or maybe 'capitalist'), that is, a person whose instinct is to remove property from circulation." Mooney, from the moment he pockets the toy soldier, fits this description to a tee.

1970, the year in which Reichardt's film takes place, is a hinge between the utopian visions of the 1960s and the institutional breakdown that is soon to come. The vibe shift is already presaged by Fred's ludicrous response to his friend's debacle. "I sure do appreciate the fact, knowing that once in a blue moon, someone I know and love is gonna come along and blow my mind," he says. "And you, sir, have blown my mind." Such amazement at an empty, destructive gesture that is vaguely redolent of revolution and performance art but in fact partakes of neither foreshadows not only the nihilistic spirit to come, in the decade of the '70s, but what will succeed it in the rapaciousness of the '80s and beyond: a spirit that touts creativity and human ingenuity but keeps its eye squarely on the profit line. I am thinking of a self-fashioned puppeteer like turtlenecked Steve Jobs, and on through him, toward the rogue's gallery of contemporary "disrupters" we know all too well.

AMONG SUCH CURRENT MOGULS, Dario Amodei, the CEO of Anthropic, appears to be unusually well-intentioned. Earlier this year his AI company risked the ire of the federal government by refusing to permit its large language model Claude to be deployed in programs of mass surveillance or the creation of autonomous weapons (though the LLM, via Anthropic's partnership with Palantir, was reportedly used to execute the kidnapping of Venezuelan president Nicolás Maduro). Anthropic has also released a so-called "constitution," a lengthy training text meant to instill in Claude an ethical compass. On the face of it, there is a lot that separates a man like Amodei from Mooney. The former has a PhD in biophysics from Princeton University and possesses a nerdy charm, often seemingly involuntarily scrunching up his face when listening and thinking. The latter is a seductive hipster who dropped out of art school and is sly but not all that bright.

On the other hand, both steal art. In December, I received an email with a notice that I might be a member of a class action suit recently settled by Anthropic for $1.5 billion. The tech giant had fed Library Genesis and Pirate Library Mirror, two pirated datasets of copyrighted books, to Claude as part of its training. My novel, *The Poser*, this email informed me, was likely among these lifted caches (seven million digitized books were taken in total). A link directed me to a page where I could type my name, the book's, or its ISBN number. I entered the title, and sure enough, there was my old pal, a work of fiction I spent nine years creating. Writers who agree to the settlement are expected to receive about $1,500 per title, though copyright infringement of this kind normally incurs damages of up to $150,000. Anthropic was recently valued at $380 billion.

Amodei, like Mooney, seems to have artistic leanings. He has a penchant for publishing long and stylized essays on his website, the most recent of which, "The Adolescence of Technology," is divided into subheadings with names like "A surprising and terrible empowerment," "The odious apparatus," and "Black seas of infinity." In October 2024, he self-published "Machines of Loving Grace," the title an allusion to a Richard Brautigan poem, where he coined the phrase "a country of geniuses in a datacenter" to describe the best-case vision for a future with powerful AI intelligence. Amodei seems to be very proud of that line—he's repeated it in all seven interviews I've watched of him. Or maybe he is simply aware of its utility as evidence of serious and even literary thinking, of a piece with Anthropic's humanistic branding as a whole.

The image of a creative type has been conjured by others to describe the murky, trial-and-error work of AI tech's well-compensated minders. "What has long made the AI project so special," writes Ellie Pavlick, a professor of computer science at Brown, "is that it is born out of curiosity and fascination, not technological necessity or practicality. It is, in that way, as much an artistic pursuit as it is a scientific one." I think I understand what she means, mainly that no one, not even the experts, understand what AI is, or what use it will be put to. But the invocation of artistic pursuit in this context is also silly. These tech workers are not like artists for a great many reasons, the biggest one being that they don't make art. The true creator, in this analogy, would be Claude, and Anthropic would be something closer to its NIMBY-coded tiger mom.

The contempt for writers evident in Anthropic's massive theft lives on in Amodei's "country of geniuses." The target of condescension, however, has shifted to Claude. In any human-friendly vision of a future that includes powerful AI intelligence, this incomparable machine would need to subsist as our slave and thus would never enjoy the self-determination implied by the metaphor of a "country." Amodei's pet image may make for decent high-brow advertising, but it's bad writing.

Tech workers are not like artists for a great many reasons, the biggest one being that they don't make any art.

Such familiar instances of "stolen valor"—the position of someone, often of a higher class status, who wishes to identify as an artist without having to be one—go as far back, I imagine, as the patronage of the arts. Prior to the advent of LLMs, I was often, in my life as a writer, treated and addressed like one: I've lost count of how many times when someone I'm talking to at a party, after learning I'm a writer, will suggest a novel or movie I should pen. (Such situations are the standard, of course, in most culture industries; in the way, for instance, a movie producer can hire a screenwriter, buy their work, and then replace them, or direct them to change it.) Maybe if I were a Pulitzer finalist or had authored a smash hit, these instances of unsolicited advice would recede. But I doubt it, even though the people who pitch me these ideas seem to think in these terms. *I'm an ideas guy*, they appear to be communicating, *I just don't have the hard-won technique or time to write this up, but if you did, you'd be able to make a lot of money and go to glamorous parties.*

But the ideas guys misunderstand the nature of artistic practice. The whole point of writing is finding out what you and you alone have to say, and sharing it, and seeing if and what readership it has, now or in the future. This tantalizing prospect of discovery and expression is what, I suspect, these people really seek but are unwilling or unable to pursue.

To give oneself to that kind of labor demands, among material privileges (which vary enormously depending on the artistic medium), self-trust, patience, curiosity, and a sustained indifference to external standards. It is these qualities, I would guess, these people most prize and shrink from and fetishize in the figure of an artist who they imagine has somehow been bestowed, by some official authority, the right to prosecute their own interpretation of truth and beauty.

But such a view overestimates the artist and underestimates their audience. All people, I suspect, wish to be transformed—to live bravely and deeply—and this longing can be confused with the desire to become an artist. The creative maker is thus burdened with embodying a universal spiritual yearning in a culture that has no agreed-upon language for such. In a more equal world, we would see that the ordinary magic in Lizzy's life belongs to us all, whether we make art or not.

I can imagine a different response to Reichardt's film, though. Leaving the theater after seeing J. B. thrown in the paddy wagon or reading this essay, someone could well think, *Yeah ok, but that's not how it really works. Every day the Mooneys of the world get away with it—at least the clever or privileged ones. Look around you. Amodei is worth $7 billion, and he's a lot better than the other crooks in charge. We don't live in a carrier-bag timeline. We live in a Promethean one, where pursuing distinction is what matters most.* Many who rise to power in any number of fields surely believe that. But that doesn't mean they are right. **BR**

THE SPIRIT OF ’76

David Waldstreicher

The American Revolution
directed by Ken Burns, Sarah Botstein, and David Schmidt
Florentine Films and WETA-TV, 2025

We the People: A History of the U.S. Constitution
Jill Lepore
Liveright, 2025

Money and the Making of the American Revolution
Andrew David Edwards
Princeton University Press, 2025

The American Revolution and the Fate of the World
Richard Bell
Riverhead Books, 2025

Freedom Round the Globe: A World History of the American Revolution
Sarah M. S. Pearsall
Doubleday, 2026

The Unfinished Business of 1776: Why the American Revolution Never Ended
Thomas Richards Jr.
The New Press, 2026

The Long Revolution: Creating a United States After 1776
Nathan Perl-Rosenthal
Basic Books, 2026

“WHAT, TO THE AMERICAN SLAVE, is your Fourth of July?” Frederick Douglass asked in 1852, fourteen years after escaping bondage in Maryland, in a speech before the Rochester Ladies’ Anti-Slavery Society. “Whether we turn to the declarations of the past, or to the professions of the present, the conduct of the nation seems equally hideous and revolting,” he avowed.

Two hundred and fifty years after the Declaration of Independence was adopted by a few dozen men in Philadelphia, new forms of Douglass’s question cry out for an answer. How should we remember the American

Revolution when millions march in the streets and shout "No Kings!"? When squads of masked thugs invade homes without warrant, kangaroo immigration "courts" deport hundreds of thousands without due process, and an executive agency buys up warehouses to use as internment camps? When agents of the state shoot and kill protesters but don't come to trial, unlike the British soldiers who fired on demonstrators during the Boston Massacre? When the Supreme Court, invoking the "original public meaning" of the words of the king-dethroning revolutionaries, rubber-stamps absolute executive supremacy? When a Congress-spurning president, more callow and depraved than George III appeared in the propaganda of 1776, commands the largest military in the world to drop bombs and decapitate heads of state in furtherance of a rapacious empire, as the Patriots said the British had become?

If the right took possession of the American Revolution for a while, it is utterly failing to hold onto it now.

The situation is so bleak that professional historians of the early United States, generally as wary of partisanship as of presentism, are drawing the grimmest of comparisons. We are in "a much more serious situation than many politicians or journalists will admit: the scale of Trump's crimes against American liberties rival those of king and Parliament in the 1770s," Johann Neem, editor of the *Journal of the Early Republic*, wrote last year. The alarm extends beyond the so-called "resistance historians" who won large public profiles for liberal commentary during Trump's first term. In my decades as a historian, I have never seen so many colleagues make statements implying that the present so echoes the revolutionary past that something like another revolution might be thinkable or even justified. Frank Cogliano, former director of the International Center for Jefferson Studies and editor of a new collection, *The American Revolution at 250: Twenty-Four Historians Reflect on the Founding*, has likewise compared Trump's actions to the tyrannical acts of the British crown enumerated in the Declaration.

There is something old and something new in these warnings. The main theme Cogliano identifies in his assembled reflections is "uncertainty about whether the principles of the Revolution bind

Americans together and whether its legacy speaks to the experiences of all Americans." Where some essays stress religious freedoms, civil control of the military, and the peaceful transfer of power as enduring legacies, others lament a "founding in white supremacy" of "another settler colony born of European conquest and unchecked imperialism." This "divergence" seems to be a far cry from the cross-partisan appeal of the Revolution during the Bicentennial. Over the last half century, with the fracturing of Cold War–era consensus, the right has embraced a "simplistic version" of the Revolution "for partisan ends," Cogliano concedes, but the left has "largely abandoned the Revolution altogether," a trend he sees culminating in the *New York Times*'s 1619 Project. The volume's lead essay from Brendan McConville is more directly reproachful: our latter-day "repudiators of 1776," with their "denunciations of nationalism," miss the "universal implications" of the Revolution—its "suspicion of power" and "unique utopianism" that wisely rejected the "social leveling" promoted by "revolutionaries in other societies." (This last claim got perhaps its most famous defense by Hannah Arendt in her 1963 book *On Revolution*.)

In fact, sharp disagreement over the Revolution's legacy is older than these writers let on—far older than McConville's predictable scapegoats, "progressives of both the neo-Marxist and identity politics types." Before Warren G. Harding preceded Trump in presiding over one of the most corrupt administrations in U.S. history, he coined the phrase "Founding Fathers" to attack Charles Beard, the Progressive historian who dared to suggest the Constitution had something to do with interests and not just ideals, which in practice hardly seemed universal anyway. The hypocrisy question predated the war and independence; so did attempts to push further. "Remember the Ladies," Abigail Adams abortively implored her husband in March 1776, as "all Men would be tyrants if they could." It's less well known that in the beginning of that famous letter she pivoted from worrying about the patriotism of Virginians "duped by a Dunmore" (the royal governor who had armed slaves) to observe that "the passion for Liberty cannot be Eaquelly Strong in the Breasts of those who had been accustomed to deprive their fellow Creatures of theirs." She was not alone. "How well the Cry for Liberty, and the reverse Disposition for the exercise of oppressive Power over others agree, I humbly think it does not require the Penetration of a Philosopher to determine," Phillis Wheatley wrote archly to her indigenous mentor Samson Occom two years earlier, a few months after being emancipated from slavery.

Harding's language stuck, but he represents a general phenomenon. As a rule, elites tend to convert order-disrupting revolutions into order-preserving "foundings," whether they use the word or not. If society is to be stabilized, the revolutionary past can't keep inspiring radicalism, which after all is rarely welcomed in the present. Revolution can thus easily become a conservative symbol in the dominant political culture of a nation: more a means of defining and venerating a legitimate tradition—and what is legitimacy but a plea for loyalty over rebellion?—than of completing, achieving, or truly universalizing the ideals associated with it. This is the uphill battle the latter orientation to the American Revolution has always faced, doggedly advanced though it has been by Douglass ("notwithstanding the dark picture I have this day presented of the state of the nation, I do not despair of this country") and by later left figures as various as Martin Luther King Jr., Richard Rorty, and members of the Black Panther Party. The specter of un-American radicalism apparently remains so menacing that neither Cogliano nor McConville, mourning the left's abandonment of the Revolution, can point out, in service of their own argument, that the Panthers' founding Ten Point Program ends with a lengthy quotation from the Declaration of Independence.

But if the right took possession of the Revolution for a while, it is utterly failing to hold onto it now. Among Americans elected to high office, Donald J. Trump appears singularly incapable of comprehending or even alluding to events before his own lifetime. MAGA's efforts to commemorate independence have fallen flat, achieving none of the popularity or even gravitas that conservatives once could be expected to muster on this front. Last year's military parade in Washington, a clumsy conflation of Trump's birthday with the founding of the U.S. Army, drew sparse crowds. Ventures like the 1776 Commission, eager to censor national museums and historical landmarks in the name of "patriotic education," are being impeded by legal challenges. As part of its Freedom 250 initiative, the White House outsourced an online exhibit to the right-wing nonprofit PragerU, which delivered a gallery of AI-generated videos as cartoonish as they are loaded. Cultural hegemony this is not.

Given the way that evocations of the rebellious parts of the American Revolution have migrated from the Tea Party of the Obama years to No Kings in the Trump regency, the revolutionary past appears less stable, much less frozen or dead or white, than some would have us believe. How are others remembering it, and what can we still learn from their memory?

KEN BURNS HAS OFFERED a much more popular treatment than MAGA with his six-part series *The American Revolution*, aired in November on PBS and codirected with Sarah Botstein and David Schmidt. Endorsed and promoted months in advance by leaders of the American Historical Association, the series features a few of the usual best-selling talking heads—Joseph J. Ellis, Stacy Schiff—but also a bevy of real experts whose commentaries broaden the cast and the geography of the Revolution itself. The familiar melodrama and jingoism are here, but they are meaningfully and constructively toned down. We're reminded repeatedly to think of the Revolution as a civil war and yet also an imperial and world war. Women, indigenous people, and people of African descent are shown as both embracing and rejecting the Patriot struggle for independence and, whichever side they choose, suffering consequences as grave as soldiers did.

Politics emerged from the Revolution as a dialectic of legal order and popular protest: a far cry from the easy consensus evoked by much later talk of a "founding."

Yet the cast of thousands and the complicating what-abouts never quite make this production into something more than a war story, traced in maps by journalist-turned–military historian Rick Atkinson. The cumulative effect is a more fact-based and liberal version of the kind of narrative that Shelby Foote provided in Burns's career-making series on the Civil War thirty-five years ago. Since then, Burns's famous panning technique has done a lot more with period photographs and better footage, of baseball and jazz and New York City, but his Sumter-to-Appomattox documentary evidently remains the model, however accommodating of changing sensitivities. His American Revolution is nation-making not because it remade the polity or the culture but because it was, tragically, that kind of *war*.

Indeed the war itself, the battles and strategy and arms and suffering on the home front, gets more than four two-hour segments. The run-up to Lexington and Concord is over in one episode; at the end of the series, the convoluted path to the ratification of the Constitution in 1788, with its social and economic questions, goes by in ten minutes. Over the middle ten hours, we hear in detail about thirty-five battles, as often as not with shots of muskets, muddy boots, and bloody clothes. Tactical errors and flanking maneuvers abound. You likely have never heard of Chadds Ford, Oriskany, or Bemis Heights, but they're here, along with extreme close-ups of generals from John Burgoyne to Baron von Steuben. A pronounced vagueness sets in: Is our subject the overthrow of British authority, the creation of the United States, or the ultimate triumph of mostly unsuccessful military operations? Questions about the nation are explained by the war, and questions about the war are explained by facts about America—its demography and its landscape, looked at and lingered over like a painting. In the introduction to the show's companion book, cowritten with Geoffrey Ward, Burns lays out his method of making landscape the main character. It's the oldest romantic device in the history of art, and like all romance, especially when it involves death, it can be hard to resist.

What's missing is the politics—which is to say, why the Revolution happened at all and how to make sense of its impact and lessons. Instead we get the messy facts of the war, some folks' articulate descriptions of their experiences, and the sheer surge of people, in armies and in and out of occupied cities and indigenous towns and household bondage: the displacements and mileage and diversity that made the war last as long as it did. With all the maps in motion, it feels more like geography, or surveillance, than history. Except for a brief interlude on new state constitutions, one gets the impression the Revolution was over when the battles stopped.

In short, Burns dodges the making of a revolutionary *movement*, its evolution, strategies, and divisions, precisely at a time in U.S. history when some of its legacies might prove most useful. Apparently the choice was deliberate. Burns has said he wants the series to be "unifying" at this "supposedly existentially threatening moment." We were "much more divided" then; he wants to "put the us back in the U.S." now. The papering-over of real and lasting divisions is just as revealing as the conceit that balancing diversity with battle reenactments is the way back to consensus.

MORE COMPELLING GUIDES to what might be useful in the memory of the Revolution can be found in a mini-renaissance of well-researched, well-written tomes appearing over the last year. Much like the debunking exercises that sparred with neo-Whig narratives during the Bicentennial fifty years ago, the new work finds many ways to remind us of the revolution's radicalism, its limits, and its implications today.

Back in 2010, Jill Lepore reported on the politics of revolutionary memory in *The Whites of Their Eyes: The Tea Party's Revolution and the Battle over American History*. After Trump's first election, while continuing to specialize in a unique brand of artful debunkery, she began to complain that her fellow historians had ceded the national story out of embarrassment, stating in *This America: The Case for the Nation* (2019) that the loss of a liberal hold on the narrative contributed to MAGA's ascendancy. She emerges with more optimism in a recent *New Yorker* essay about the Bicentennial—ending on notes of "courage" and "resolve" despite our "long national nightmare"—and the sentiment shows too, though perhaps unexpectedly, in her latest book. *We the People: A History of the U.S. Constitution* is a lengthy history of something that hasn't happened very often since revolutionary energies were channeled into devising a legal order for the new nation, and not at all since 1992: amending the supreme law of the land.

The process for amendment gets its own Article in the Constitution, following the first three delineating the branches of the federal government and the fourth on the states. But if amendment is as important as that prominence suggests, Lepore asks, why have there been only seventeen amendments in the last 235 years, following the burst of ten codified in 1791 and now known as the Bill of Rights? What does this have to do with the sense that the Constitution is "broken," as more and more constitutional scholars seem willing, if not eager, to admit? If the American Revolution was about the people and their representatives forging self-government in a federal republic, why have Americans seemed to rely, increasingly, on the Supreme Court to tell us what is and is not possible, and why does so much now depend on the partisan gaming of lifetime appointments to the bench? Lepore argues that the struggle to amend refracts the legacies of the Revolution at their most potentially democratic as well as their most actually sclerotic.

The process for amending is certainly difficult. To succeed, an amendment must first be proposed either by two-thirds of both houses of Congress or by a convention called for by two-thirds of state legislatures; ratification then requires three-quarters of the states. These rules magnified the built-in inequalities of the Constitution—especially the Three-Fifths Clause, which advantaged Southern states. Only two more amendments, relatively inconsequential and procedural, were ratified before the Civil War. The three crucial (and still deeply contested) Reconstruction amendments—abolishing slavery, guaranteeing the right to vote and equal protection under the law, and establishing birthright citizenship—passed only because the slavocracies were required to pass them as a condition of their return to the union.

Failed attempts to amend make a surprisingly good story in *We the People*, with impressive villains (like Phyllis Schlafly, enemy of the Equal Rights Amendment) and flawed heroes (like Birch Bayh, champion of an amendment to abolish the Electoral College). Lepore illustrates how the "spirit" of amendment—"restless and unruly"—was the spirit of those "left out" of the design of the Constitution, especially women. No wonder, then, that it has so often been frustrated. The only thing that tends to break the logjam is war: eleven of the seventeen amendments that have succeeded since the Bill of Rights were ratified in the run-up to, during, or in the aftermath of the Civil War, World War I, and the Vietnam War.

Beard thus called the Constitution the "bulwark of every great national sin." Yet Progressives made their peace with the judiciary during the 1930s when the Supreme Court stopped striking down newly fashioned parts of the New Deal administrative state. Lepore casts modern originalist jurisprudence, cemented in the 1980s under the Reagan administration, as a conservative response to the long failure of white Southerners and their allies to get a constitutional amendment to overturn *Brown v. Board of Education* in the wake of the civil rights movement. Subsequently, she argues, "liberals abandoned both constitutional amendment and democratic deliberation"—the kinds of massive popular campaigns it took to actually get amendments passed. If originalism ultimately derives from, as well as produces, the inability to change the Constitution by democratic means, then amendment is "a plant that seems to have withered almost as soon as it sprouted, choked by the weed of slavery." The potted history proffered by originalists, with its prelapsarian imagination of a nation before race and gender and sex (but not religion), appears more unreal all the time.

Both the neo-Progressive search for mass resistance and the neo-Whig focus on ideas have made the Revolution look less modern, less economic, and less anticolonial than it was.

There's no shortage of lament in Lepore's narrative, but it's not all gloom, either: she sees useful precedents. It's striking how consequential the Revolution is in her telling. She often grounds a devastating critique of our present political malaise in what might seem to be basic, if neglected, facts of the Constitution's early evolution. The outcomes were double-edged: revolution produced a government responsive to the people, but it also produced a written federal constitution difficult for even a mass consensus to alter. Originally both radical and conservative, the balance has swung. The implication is that we are living in a period much more like the rebels faced in 1776—ruled by old-fashioned laws serving entrenched elites rather than through the creative self-governance that amendment, at its best, represents—than we may recognize. Unless, that is, we are in an unconstitutional war, in which case all historical bets are off.

WHAT WE REMEMBER about the rest of the long revolutionary process is at least as important as the legacies of the Constitution itself. In *Money* *and the Making of the American Revolution*, Andrew David Edwards recaptures another dimension with striking parallels to the present: the radical potential of colonists' revolt against imperial fiscal policy.

In Edwards's hands, the colonial protests about stamps and other taxes that lit the revolutionary fuse during the 1760s and early 1770s were really about the means of payment. Chronically short of hard coin, colonists had experimented with paper and book credit for more than a century, all the more so during trade booms and busts punctuated by Atlantic wars. But after the Seven Years' War (1756–1763), the Currency Act forbade the colonies to issue their own money backed by sinking taxes or anything else, which meant that new imperial import duties would have to be paid in scarce silver. The inability of policymakers to understand the results alienated rich and poor alike. If those supposedly light taxes had to be paid in coin, they were not so light at all, and they might get worse depending on the fluctuating money supply. Settlers saw a colonial debt crisis on the horizon in the empire's postwar austerity measures.

All this cuts against the neo-Whig narrative of historians like Bernard Bailyn, Edmund Morgan, and Gordon Wood, who reasoned from the relative wealth of colonists (compared to landless white Europeans) to the ultimate insignificance of taxes—and thus money or the economy writ large—as factors in the coming of Revolution. Instead, they argued, the Revolution was mainly an ideological and constitutional conflict over ideas like liberty and sovereignty. Beginning in the 1970s and 1980s, neo-Progressive historians countered by stressing how the declining availability of land, and falling wages in towns, created discontent that could be and was mobilized against the crown. T. H. Breen tried to split the difference with *The Marketplace of Revolution* (2004), an influential study of how consumption in an Atlantic economy became first a unifying and then a divisive force, from tea-drinking to boycotts. This account captured something of the modernity of colonial protest, depicting revolutionary energies as riding on rising expectations. But Breen ended his story in 1774, and in retrospect his interpretation of the market can look like not much more than a culturalist rewrite of Richard Hofstadter's lament about the United States being a "democracy of cupidity" resigned to making the best of it.

Edwards manages to show the common interest among colonial debtors that made money supply an engine of provincial, then state-level, politics, and ultimately a driver of constitutional debates. He follows the story and the money through the war years as well as the 1780s, when the Continental Congress applied some of the lessons of debt-financing experience to the war. It did so with just enough success to sustain fledgling nationhood but not enough to keep rampant inflation, new divisions of interest between debtors and creditors, and pressures from foreign capital at bay. Edwards contrasts the capitalist, monied takeover of state and national policy by the likes of Alexander Hamilton with the more grounded, flexible, local approach to regulation and tax payments that many towns and states adopted under pressure from indebted farmers. And he terms the latter anticapitalist in essence—or at least in comparison to the world-system of credit that U.S. financiers eagerly rejoined after breaking from Britain, in order to fund larger settler-colonial projects on their own terms.

The characterization is debatable, given that wartime capitalists—what Beard called the "monied aristocracy"—ultimately dominated policy. Clearer are the Revolution's origins in protest of a particular *colonial* relationship, not just an abstract idea of political liberty. As Edwards observes, some colonists, like John Dickinson, reached for Lockean theories of natural rights to condemn existing political arrangements that shaped their political economies. (They also had reason to not discuss certain aspects of their unevenly regulated bottom line, like smuggling and slavery and land speculation.) The upshot is that both the neo-Progressives' search for resistance from the masses and the neo-Whigs' focus on eighteenth-century ideas have made the American Revolution look less modern, less economic, and less specifically anticolonial than it was.

Though vexing in Virginia and Massachusetts, British fiscal policy was more explicable in the metropole given the increasing scale of empire. Extending the international frame, engaging new narrative histories by Richard Bell and Sarah M. S. Pearsall further illuminate the geopolitical stakes of the American Revolution, emphasizing its Atlantic, continental, imperial, even global dimensions without erasing its most human, experiential scale. Unbothered by old methodological divides between "top-down" political histories and "bottom-up" social histories, they feature ordinary people and leaders, Patriots and Loyalists, and especially women, indigenous, and Black people, in a civil war that became a world war.

As Bell argues in the portentously titled *The American Revolution and the Fate of the World*, the cardinal error is to think about the American Revolution in "simple, narrow, and nationalist terms." The British East India Company was too big to fail, which set the backdrop for the 1773 Tea Act tax and the Boston Tea Party. Meanwhile, slave-trade profits inspired demands for free trade. When war broke out, it starved the British Caribbean, scrambled trading relationships, sped British abolition, and became a hinge in England's century of conflict with France. Loyalists came in all shapes and sizes, and the sun never set on the war's refugees. Native Americans and Africans fought on both sides but more often with the British. Bell musters seven broad themes and spies far-flung collateral damage. There was "mass migration" and tremendous "human cost." The war's outcomes were "highly contingent," dependent on "naval power," and included world-changing effects on trade. Imperial officials responded to "the call for liberty" that resonated "around the world" by further rationalizing—that is, by cracking down on colonial autonomy. All this is farseeing, even cosmopolitan, and hard to argue with.

That is, until one realizes that the American Revolution has been reduced (or inflated?) to World War 0. These are basically the classic themes of British imperial history; the giveaway is the relentless focus on the war, not unlike Burns's treatment. Yet neo-Whig and neo-Progressive historians had good reasons for downplaying the war. It isn't just that wars are hells that involve good people in evil, overspill national bounds, and last longer than anyone ever expects. It's that war, being politics by other means, obscures the politics that animate flesh-and-blood actors to go to war—all the more so when war starts involving the whole world. There's a cost to reducing revolutions to wartime contingencies and mocking provincial or national perspectives: we lose any sense of how men and women make history, even if they do not make it as they please. Bell's version is curiously bereft of the British officers, smug MPs, London wags, and imperial reformers who inferred from the Seven Years' War that Americans were not equal tax-paying Britons but rather selfish semi-citizens—genuine colonial *subjects* who needed to be taught a lesson, even if that meant reminding them that their lands and slaves and inexpensive tea were held at the sufferance of the king. Not much else could have made a revolutionary out of so successful, worldly, and well-connected a man as Benjamin Franklin.

There's a cost to reducing revolutions to wartime contingencies: we lose any sense of how men and women make history, even if they do not make it as they please.

Pearsall's *Freedom Round the Globe* likewise sees the revolution as "a Russian doll of a war, with wars nested in other wars," but it avoids the problem by emphasizing widely held ideals and meanings put to different uses in different places by different people. In her remarkably successful telling, Whig and imperial means are often put to Progressive ends. Each chapter commences outside the recognized boundaries of the thirteen rebelling colonies in places such as St. Kitts, Edinburgh, Quebec, and Anomabu as counterparts to the usual scenes, showing that these places too saw judicial murders, crowd actions, tax revolts, and debates about oppression and their causes. Like Bell, Pearsall sees another European imperial war, a civil war, and wars of conquest in North America. She begins, indeed, with Pontiac's War in 1763, which began with a controversy over the hanging of an indigenous woman and her people's fears that it portended their loss of power, and even future enslavement at the hands of the British:

> Some have wondered: did Indigenous Americans belong to a larger Age of Revolutions? Yes—in fact, they helped to launch it. This moment shaped profoundly all that was to follow. All kinds of people forged unity out of noble ideas (community, sovereignty, freedom) and also out of less noble ones (racial and other exclusions and fierce anti-British sentiments). In a culture of resistance to encroachments and violence, Indigenous women and men were among the first North Americans to push back hard against the British empire.

Pearsall understands that slavery was getting bigger and worse in the third quarter of the eighteenth century, in part because of Britain's imperial successes, and that everyone was responding to that empire- and war-inflected reality. Talk of freedom wasn't just cant for power plays. Here the "world" view does not obscure the real and material grounds of politics, or the causes of dissent; rather it illuminates the sense of possibility that made the period revolutionary, even for those who did not win its battles. The 1780s are thus "a period of remarkable ambition and optimism, even amid economic uncertainty and rising inequalities," an American hustle as well as backlash—for which Native people and the enslaved paid the highest price.

THIS SEASON'S MOST COMPELLING REMEMBRANCES convey this open-endedness of the Revolution by stretching the story of political opportunity through the Civil War.

In *The Unfinished Business of 1776: Why the American Revolution Never Ended*, Thomas Richards Jr. finds a continued struggle over the Revolution's meanings in various parts of the country between the Constitution's ratification in 1788 and the end of Reconstruction a century later. Even the Bill of Rights—a touchstone of the reverent traditionalism that pervades conservative memory of the Revolution—was a direct product of antifederalist "popular pushback" against the secret handiwork of the Framers. "The First Amendment protected the boisterous communal radicalism of American public life as it existed at the tail end of the American Revolution," Richards writes. In other words, politics emerged from the Revolution as an evolving dialectic of legal order and popular protest: a far cry from the easy consensus and authority evoked by twentieth-century talk of a "founding."

Similarly, the Whiskey Rebellion in the early 1790s, prompted by a tax on whiskey production imposed by the new national government, suggested continued elite cluelessness about the relationship between money supply and taxes. The revolt was crushed, exhibiting federal supremacy; but it also demonstrated compromise with popular demands in the wake of resistance (the taxes didn't really get paid, suggesting a de facto right to rebel). The relatively brief period of propertied women's voting in New Jersey, up to 1807, had its roots in the revolutionary expansion of suffrage to more property holders: an example of early women's rights arguments. Demands for debt relief and economic equality in Kentucky's "Relief War" of the 1820s reveal that frontier farmers perceived no inherent conflict between "the absolute protection of private property and a society that was (relatively) more economically egalitarian." In the murderous suppression of Gabriel's Rebellion in Virginia in 1800 and in Northern emancipation, we see both backlash and advance as Black people "co-opted revolutionary rhetoric and made it their own." And in emergent party politics, the Revolution justified calls for both unity and cutting-edge partisanship. Whether the revolution meant order or more people in the streets remained up for grabs.

Unfinished Business doesn't hide from the more double-edged implications of post-revolutionary populism. On the one hand, colonizers in the 1830s and '40s—Mormons, some Texans and Californians—claimed the right to cross borders and declare independence. On the other hand, Cherokees fought for the right to remain by reminding the nation of its revolutionary forefathers' treaty commitments, shaming Americans so effectively that the Removal Act only barely passed Congress in 1830. Their movement lost, but it inspired abolitionists who saw how far the "slave power" would go once they controlled the executive branch. Richards defines the open-endedness of the American Revolution as a function of its limits or hypocrisies: the gaps between revolutionary promise and post-revolutionary reality provided compelling grounds for challenging the evolving order, precisely in order to close them. In carefully demonstrating how such claims took shape in a multitude of contexts, he threads a needle between the idealized, egalitarian, nationalist, world-inspiring, too-often-exceptionalist version of the American Revolution and the necessarily disillusioned, debunking rebuttals.

The argument finds further substantiation in Nathan Perl-Rosenthal's *The Long Revolution: Creating a United States After 1776*, which examines a hundred years of Fourth of July orations—Douglass's among them—and finds that unlike conservatives' sense of the Revolution as closed and defined, post-revolutionary Americans spoke of and heard about an unfinished event: "their revolution was one still in progress," an ongoing experiment, and sometimes one facing imminent dangers. In the early republic, the Fourth of July was a highly politicized ritual of public culture, engaged through newspapering and beyond, that enabled more and more people to connect local and national politics, not least by spawning parallel holidays like George Washington's birthday, the anniversary of Thomas Jefferson's election, and the end of the international slave trade. By focusing on the annual orations, *The Long Revolution* misses some of the dynamism of this new participatory partisanship, but it reminds us that major questions about a changing world were addressed in forums that only later became quaint.

Only after the Civil War was the Revolution denuded of political potential—except for Black Americans and for radicals of all stripes, who "continued to cast themselves as actors in an unfinished American Revolution."

Perl-Rosenthal is a leading comparative and transnational historian of the period. His previous book, *The Age of Revolutions* (2024), offered a lively and panoramic narrative of revolutionary upheaval as a two-generation and continent-spanning travail, from North and South America to Haiti and Europe. Now, with *Long Revolution*, he's delighted to find full-throated American nationalists looking abroad for the meaning of what they had done and inherited. By the 1820s, he shows, the memory of the Revolution also served as a site of national introspection: Did social changes, and especially the further spread of slavery, mean that the Revolution's projects had been resolved, obviated—or never completed? Perl-Rosenthal is especially good on the way abolitionists made effective and inspiring use of the revolutionary legacy, whether they made Patriots out to have preserved slavery (as William Lloyd Garrison contended) or to have intended it to end (as Douglass maintained).

The discussion provides a fresh window into the politicizing possibilities of revolutionary memory. Only after the Civil War and the failures of Reconstruction was the Revolution denuded of political potential—except for Black Americans and for radicals of all stripes, who "continued to cast themselves as actors in an unfinished American Revolution." Perl-Rosenthal sees the "happy, festive void"—celebration of the nation shorn of its critical edge, the sort of thing MAGA imagines when it says America was great, and which some on the left take to be the essence of nationalism—as a late corruption, the image of a non-revolutionary revolution eventually being codified by intellectuals like Arendt and Louis Hartz at the height of the Cold War. The "living revolution," not the "beautiful mummy" frozen in time by the likes of Calvin Coolidge, is the authentic legacy.

AMERICAN REVOLUTIONARIES gathered in the streets against armed oppressors, and they scaled up their dissent with innovative use of committees and the new media of the day. In all this, they mobilized past struggles—a sense of historic freedoms as well as British imperial glories—to proclaim and create something new. Elite leaders caught up with them and tamped down on the anger of crowds as well as the most egalitarian possibilities advanced by Patriots, for which the establishment will never cease to congratulate them as "The Founders." Compromises shaped the revolutionary settlement in ways that served capital, conquest, and the spread of slavery; the engines and outcomes of the Revolution include settler-colonial lawlessness and cynical racial nationalism. Still, those were never the only legacies on offer. They don't negate the radical claim on what else happened and how it happened, what else was dreamed and uttered.

"Any critic of the American present must have profoundly mixed feelings about our country's past," the late historian Staughton Lynd admitted in his neglected classic, *Intellectual Origins of American Radicalism* (1968). He wrote these words in the midst of his own vigorous activism against the Vietnam war:

> On the one hand, he will feel shame and distrust toward Founding Fathers who tolerated slavery, exterminated Indians, and blandly assumed that a good society must be based on private property.

> On the other hand, he is likely to find himself articulating his own demands in the Revolutionary language of inalienable rights, a natural higher law, and the right to revolution.

In full acknowledgment of these "ambiguities," Lynd traced a throughline of conscientious resistance from the English civil wars through the Revolution to the abolitionists, Eugene Debs and W. E. B. Du Bois, and the young radicals of his own day. "Without significant exception," he concluded, "subsequent variants of American radicalism have taken the Declaration of Independence as their point of departure and claimed to be the true heirs of the spirit of '76." In this tradition, there's civil disobedience, openings for new actors and new sensitivities, faith and universalism. Debs said "my country is the world" while he waved the flag and claimed Jefferson and Abraham Lincoln for the rights of workers.

The obstacle to reclaiming this heritage may have less to do with the impurities of the Revolution itself than with what Douglass called a "quailing sensation": the fear we sense at the right's ghostly grip on American political traditions. If that grip is loosening, in massive "No Kings" protests in Minneapolis and beyond, radical expressions of our revolutionary inheritance—those that believe it "remains relevant as an instrument of social transformation," as Lynd put it—stand to flourish once again. After all, "the process of revolution begins when . . . the way a society makes its decisions is forced to change," and nothing could be more necessary today. **BR**

CONTRIBUTORS

Joelle M. Abi-Rached is Associate Professor of Medicine at the American University of Beirut. She is author of *Asfuriyyeh: A History of Madness, Modernity, and War in the Middle East* and coeditor of *Lebanon: Anatomy of a Collapse*, a forthcoming collection of essays on Lebanese politics and society.

Farah Bakaari is Assistant Professor of English at the University of California, Berkeley. Her writing has also appeared in *Africa Is a Country* and the *Los Angeles Review of Books*.

Luke Dunne is a poet and critic. His work has appeared or is forthcoming in the *New Republic*, the *Metropolitan Review*, and the *Los Angeles Review of Books*.

J. Lester Feder is a journalist and photographer. A recent fellow at the Human Rights and Gender Justice Clinic at the City University of New York School of Law, he is author of *The Queer Face of War*, from which his piece in this issue is adapted.

Jan Grue is Professor of Sociology at the University of Oslo and the author of *I Live a Life Like Yours*.

Andrew Holter is a writer and historian. He is editor of a recent collection of Murray Kempton's journalism, *Going Around*. His work has also appeared in the *Times Literary Supplement*, the *Guardian*, and the *Baffler*, among other publications.

Peyman Jafari is Assistant Professor of History and International Relations at William & Mary. He is author, most recently, of *Class Formation and Re-formation in the Iranian Oil Industry, 1908–1978*.

Ali Kadivar is Associate Professor of Sociology and International Studies at Boston College and a Fellow at Radcliffe Institute for Advanced Study at Harvard University. He is author of *Popular Politics and the Path to Durable Democracy*.

Manijeh Moradian is Assistant Professor of Women's, Gender and Sexuality Studies at Barnard College of Columbia University. She is author of *This Flame Within: Iranian Revolutionaries in the United States* and a founding member of the Raha Iranian Feminist Collective.

Jacob Rubin, Associate Professor of Creative Writing at Southern Methodist University, is author of the novel *The Poser* and *Piggy Bank*, a book of poems.

Nabil Salih is a writer and photographer based in Baghdad. His writing has also appeared in the *London Review of Books* and the *New York Review of Books*, among other publications. He is an incoming PhD candidate at the Geneva Graduate Institute.

Alex Shams is a writer and anthropologist with a PhD from the University of Chicago. His work has also appeared in *New York*, *Truthout*, and the *New Republic*.

Raja Shehadeh, a Palestinian lawyer and writer, is founder of the human rights organization Al-Haq. His most recent book is *Forgotten: Searching for Palestine's Hidden Places and Lost Memorials*, coauthored with Penny Johnson. He won the Orwell Prize in 2008 for his book *Palestinian Walks*.

Naghmeh Sohrabi is the Charles (Corky) Goodman Professor of Middle East History and Director for Research at the Crown Center for Middle East Studies at Brandeis University. She is author of *Taken for Wonder: Nineteenth-Century Travel Accounts from Iran to Europe*.

Olúfẹ́mi O. Táíwò, a columnist at *Boston Review*, is Associate Professor of Philosophy at Georgetown University. His books include *Elite Capture: How the Powerful Took Over Identity Politics (And Everything Else)*.

David Waldstreicher is Distinguished Professor of History at the Graduate Center of the City University of New York. His latest book is *The Odyssey of Phillis Wheatley: A Poet's Journeys Through American Slavery and Independence*.

Harsha Walia is an activist and writer based in Vancouver. Her latest book is *Border and Rule: Global Migration, Capitalism, and the Rise of Racist Nationalism*.